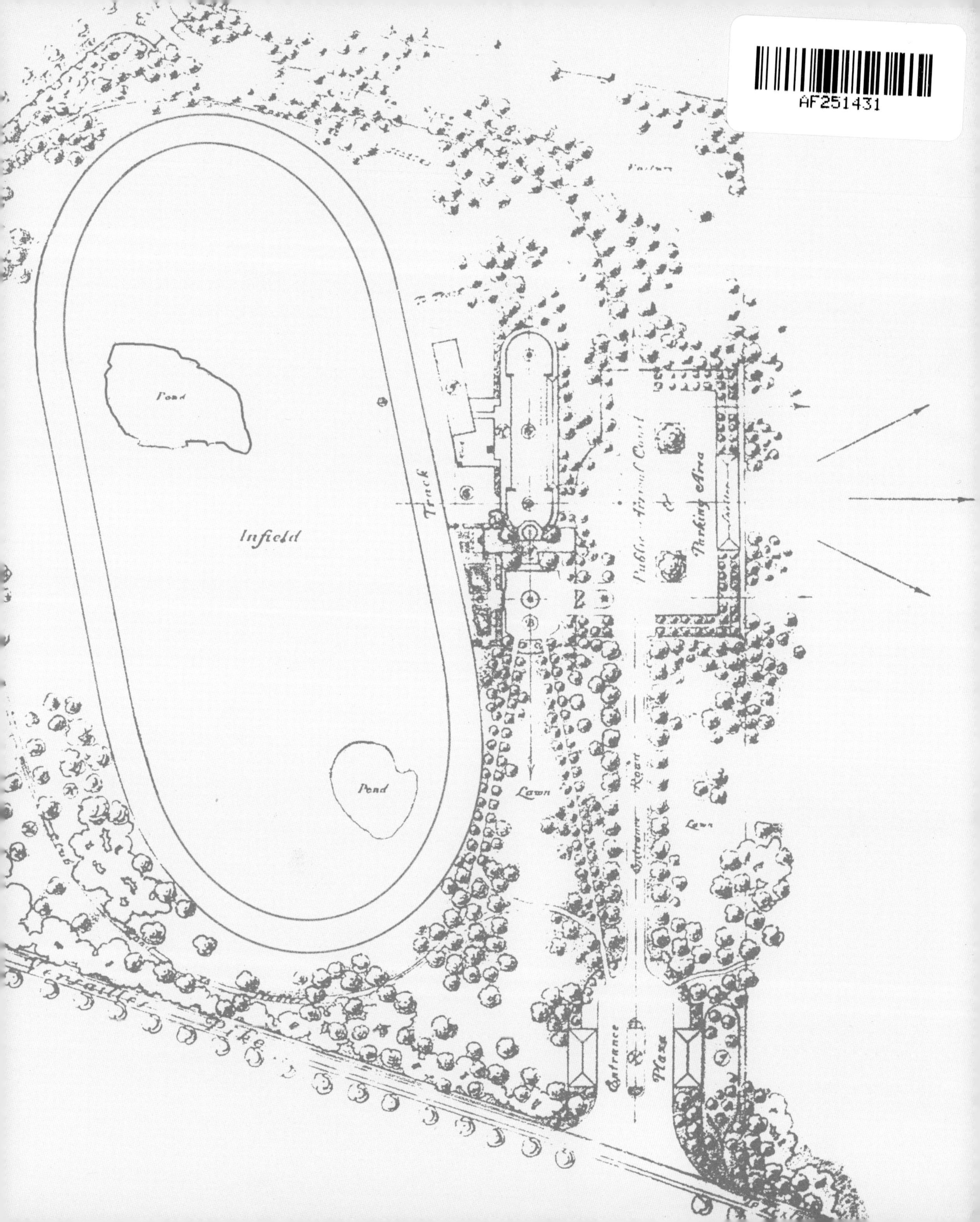

Pond
Infield
Track
Pond
Lawn
Public Arrival Court
Parking Area
Lawn
Entrance Road
Entrance Plaza
AF251431

KEENELAND

A THOROUGHBRED LEGACY

Editor, Jacqueline Duke
Concept, Project Direction, and Photo Procurement by Fran Taylor
Jacket and Book Design by Brian Turner

Library of Congress Control Number: 2009941423

ISBN 978-1-58150-334-0

Printed in China
First Edition: 2010

a division of
Blood-Horse Publications
PUBLISHERS SINCE 1916
WWW.ECLIPSEPRESS.COM

Keeneland Association
LEXINGTON, KENTUCKY 40588-1690
WWW.KEENELAND.COM

KEENELAND

A THOROUGHBRED LEGACY

TELETIMER
RACE 7
RACE 7
SCR
KEENELAND

CONTENTS

FOREWORD

By Nick Nicholson

CELEBRATING 75 YEARS OF TRADITION

Keeneland's values are timeless.

THE NIGHT BEFORE I WAS NAMED president and CEO of the Keeneland Association, Susan and I sat down with our children to tell them that our family's world was about to change. As we talked, each of us discussed what came to mind when thinking about Keeneland.

I was quickly struck by the fact that everyone's experience was different. From a morning breakfast to dressing up in our best suit or dress to the thrill of a race and the fun of being around such beautiful animals, each experience, no matter how diverse, was no less special, no less unique. Each was indelibly etched into our minds as a special time in our family's life.

Of course, our values — Keeneland values — are timeless. They don't shift with the passing sentiment of the moment. From our inception we've used every inch of our rolling, bucolic hills to invest in the betterment and health of our industry. We've used our proceeds to make racing better and our Central Kentucky community stronger. And while remaining steadfastly loyal to tradition, we've been innovative, from making our racing surfaces safer for riders and horses to leading the way in technology on-line and in the sales pavilion.

At the same time, people from all walks of life, with a broad diversity of backgrounds and experiences, bring different perceptions to Keeneland when they come, but they all walk away knowing they've been part of something special.

One of the things I cherish about Keeneland is walking the grounds in the morning, with the trainers closely watching their horses breezing or galloping; the clockers and riders going through their paces; the grounds crews and track superintendants working with great care to maintain the courses.

And as the sun begins to break through the morning mist, I try to imagine in my mind's eye what people through the generations have experienced here: Eddie Arcaro and Pat Day on their mounts; fans witnessing Whirlaway, Alydar, and Spectacular Bid thundering down the stretch; a great moment of suspense as bidders vie for that special yearling or broodmare that will serve as the foundation for future generations.

Or it could be the simple pleasure of a family together on a crisp, fall day, enjoying each other, enjoying Keeneland.

Finally, I always think back to the decisions of our founders, their legacy, and how it obliges those of us who are stewards of this place to carry on. They chose risk over comfort. In the throes of a global depression, they stayed vigilant in adhering to a vision and a set of values in creating the grounds, facilities, and ambiance that would become the industry's leader in racing and sales. Certain values and certain ideals, they knew then, aren't as easily priced or weighed as commodities.

Today those founders speak to us still, their voices echoing over lush green fields through the passages of time and history. They tell us to continue on. Our heritage — their legacy — offers testament to that vision as we embark on our next seventy-five years.

Nick Nicholson is current President and CEO of the Keeneland Asociation.

FOREWORD

By William C. "Bill" Greely

CELEBRATING 75 YEARS OF TRADITION

Keeneland to me is my home away from home!

MY IMMEDIATE FAMILY has worked for, won races, or bought and sold horses at Keeneland since 1937. My grandfather won the first race ever run for two-year-olds at Keeneland during the spring meet in 1937.

In 1946, my family arrived at Fort Springs Farm, which is now office to trainer John T. Ward just across Rice Road opposite the rear entrance to Keeneland. I was all of eight years old and my brother, Bud, was ten; Keeneland was our playground.

In 1955, at age sixteen, I asked for and was given a summer job on Keeneland's maintenance crew by the then track superintendent, Hobert Burton. For the fall of 1963 and spring meet of 1964 I was given the position of entry clerk working in the racing office in the mornings and for the director of publicity, J. B. Falconer, in the afternoons. I watched Northern Dancer win the Blue Grass Stakes that spring. In 1970, I returned to Keeneland from working as a racing official in New Jersey and Pennsylvania to become the assistant racing secretary. The racing secretary suffered a heart attack on opening day and I was asked by Keeneland's president, Ted Bassett, and general manager, W. T. Bishop, if I would run that meeting as racing secretary for Keeneland, which I was honored to do. In 1972, I was contacted by Ted Bassett and asked if I would be interested in returning to Keeneland as general manager. That was a no-brainer — no more traveling as a racing secretary; moving six times per year with my wife, children, and high chairs, baby beds, et al. We were gypsies on the road no more. We were coming home to Keeneland and Lexington at long last.

In time, my two sons, Sean and Kevin, worked on the maintenance crew and later as racing officials, and daughter, Kara, worked in the general office in the summers while in high school. My wife, Norma, opened the Keeneland Paddock Gift Ship in 1991 and operated it until our retirement in 2000.

To have worked with the likes of Ted Bassett, Stan Jones, Jim Williams, and a bit later, Rogers Beasley, made work a pleasure. We worked together as a team. To be able to come to work in a park-like setting daily and love each and every day encouraged us to think more clearly and to always do what was best for the industry.

To me, Keeneland is everything — the epitome of racing and horse sales. It is Utopia Downs! The management and facilities put the horse first in all matters. It is where traditions are treasured, passed from one generation to another to be maintained and to be improved. As has been said many times, Keeneland will never be finished and is to be enjoyed by all who choose to enter its park-like facilities.

William C. "Bill" Greely is a former general manager and president of Keeneland, where he served from 1972–2000.

FOREWORD

By James E. "Ted" Bassett

It's all about the people.

THERE IS SOMETHING MAGICAL about the mere mention of Keeneland. It casts an essence of difference, a different philosophy, a different perception. For over forty years I have experienced a certain spark of anticipation whenever I entered its gates. Whether it is the joy kindled by the faces of the Keeneland family, the ambience of the cultured landscape, or the exhilaration of the event in progress, Keeneland has the aura of a sanctuary with endless opportunity.

Upon reflection, that which makes Keeneland most special to me is the people, the whole range of interesting names and faces from here and abroad, from backside to front side, a myriad of personalities who make our racing world so unique. Keeneland seems to cast a spell over those of us fortunate enough to be associated with it, and over time it tends to become part of one's persona. For me it has been a special privilege of association, one that I shall treasure forever.

James E. "Ted" Bassett III is a former president, chairman of the board, and trustee of Keeneland, where he served from 1969–2007

KEENE FAMILY LEGACY

Vickie Mitchell

Keeneland's main entrance is marked by low walls of mortared stone, shaded by trees that thrive in the Kentucky soil and add color to the carefully tended landscape — flowering dogwoods and redbuds for the spring meet; colorful oak, maple, and other hardwoods for fall racing. At the end of the wide asphalt avenue, two-tenths of a mile long and shaded by an allee of maples, stands its clubhouse, built of the same Kentucky limestone as the rock walls that mark the racecourse's front boundary.

It is a masterfully orchestrated arrival, completely in tune with the more than 1,000 acres of Kentucky countryside that Keeneland encompasses. Such a well-groomed and carefully planned setting makes it hard to remember that Keeneland's beginnings owe much to chance and serendipity. But what many have forgotten and others never knew is that it took a dreamer, the Great Depression, and a cadre of determined and dedicated horsemen to build a racetrack so original.

Jack Keene's vision helped define Keeneland.

The story begins with John Oliver "Jack" Keene, a Lexington-born horseman, adventurer, and visionary who laid the foundation for what would become Keeneland.

With or without Keene, Lexington would have a racecourse. After all, it has been the epicenter of the Thoroughbred industry since the late 1800s. But without Keene, the racetrack would not sit six miles west of Main Street on the edge of a ridge, its clubhouse and grandstand facing Kentucky hills and the setting sun.

Keene's dream of building a training and racing facility for himself and his friends, his obsession with stone construction, and his travels around the world were the basic ingredients for what would become a National Historic Landmark and one of the world's most beautiful racetracks.

PROMINENT FAMILY

If ever the term "old Lexington" fit a family, it was the Keenes. Jack Keene's great-great grandfather, Francis Keen, was a Virginia gentleman who arrived in Fayette County in the late 1700s with a land grant awarded him by Virginia governor Benjamin Harrison.

The grant was for land near the Licking River in what is now Montgomery County, but apparently Keen preferred the rolling countryside west of Lexington and began buying tracts there. No one seems to know how much land he ultimately purchased, although it is said his holdings extended from where Keeneland is today to Lexington's city limits.

Regardless, Keen was a significant landholder, and he and his family became active members of the growing community. Son Sanford, who may have added an "e" to the end of the family name, opened Keene's Tavern, which eventually burned to be rebuilt as Lexington's Phoenix Hotel. Son John married Mary Bowman, of another prominent local family. Her father, Colonel Abraham Bowman, was a Revolutionary War commander.

The Keens' prominence in the community was most apparent on May 15, 1825. America had invited Marquis de Lafayette, the Frenchman who had aided the patriots during the Revolutionary War, now sixty-eight, to visit. His tour of the United States brought him to Lexington, where he had friends and where the county, Fayette, had been named in his honor.

There were no better Kentuckians to host Lafayette's visit than the Keens. John Keen's father-in-law Colonel Abraham Bowman had served with General Lafayette during the Revolution (not Major John Keene as noted in the historic marker) and was his good friend. John and Mary's home, Keen Place, built around 1805 was within easy reach just off the Versailles Pike.

Throngs of townspeople stood on the Keens' front lawn to greet Lafayette and his men. General Leslie Combs, a lawyer and orator who had fought in the War of 1812, introduced Lafayette to the crowd. Unruly children were likely to have been put in their place by Combs, known for using his hickory-stick cane to get the attention of the inattentive.

A room was readied for Lafayette's stay upstairs in the Keen home and the elderly Frenchman slept in a four-poster bed that the family has cherished for generations and is still using today. His men made camp on the rolling front lawn.

JACK KEENE: DREAMER AND VISIONARY

Remarkably, Keene Place still stands, shrouded from modern-day traffic on Versailles Road by the more than 1,000 trees that surround it. One of the oldest homes in Lexington, it is now owned by the Keeneland Association and has been painstakingly restored. The project began in 2003, took six years, and involved

Keene Place welcomed famous visitors such as the Marquis de Lafayette; below, right, Jack Keene was a skilled horseman and dapper dresser.

Keene's boyhood home underwent extensive reonvations after its purchase by Keeneland.

experts from the University of Kentucky Center for Historic Architecture and Preservation. Among the new paintings commissioned for the home are two that salute Jack Keene and his impact on the Thoroughbred industry.

One shows the 1914 Belmont winner Luke McLuke, who stood at stud at Keene's farm; the other is of Alice Blue Gown, one of Keene's best broodmares, with her groom, Buck Jackson, Keene's longtime employee who did everything from delivering foals to serving meals at Keene's farm.

True to its name, Keene Place was home to Keens and Keenes for several generations. Jack, born in 1870, was among them, one of four children of John and Zeruiah Keene.

By Jack Keene's day, Lexington was no longer the frontier, yet his spirited lifestyle and globetrotting travels echoed those of his pioneer ancestors.

Keene's need for adventure would eventually take him to Europe, Russia, and the Far East during an age when world travel was not as easy or as common as it is today.

Early on, horses became his passion, a natural fit for a man whose great-great grandfather had launched a Bluegrass Thoroughbred breeding operation in the late 1700s, advertising the stallion Don Careless for a stud fee of five dollars.

Keene is said to have struck out for Chicago at age twenty, with twenty dollars in his pocket. He found work with a trainer there, and a year later he became a trainer himself.

By the early 1900s he had convinced his younger brother George Hamlet "Ham" to follow the same path. Ham was his brother's opposite, grounded and conservative. The ups and downs of the Thoroughbred business made Ham nervous, yet as he stood behind a plow in a cornfield on a hot summer day and listened to his brother expound on the possibilities a racing life offered, Ham swallowed his fears and joined Jack in training and breeding partnership.

Jack Keene seemed to have luck with racing from the start. He was twenty-seven when he bought his first racehorse, a campaigner named Incetatus, named for Caligula's favorite horse; Incetatus was a winner the first time he raced under Keene's orange and black silks. Later, Keene and partner Lewis Ryan bought Braw Lad, who lived up to his tough-guy name, winning about forty races and becoming, many said, the foundation of Keene's stable.

In the early 1900s Jack Keene's worldwide wanderings began, a series of journeys that would give him international celebrity as he stirred up several controversies in other countries. His first stop was Russia, where, over the course of two trips and two years, he trained for banker Henri Bloch and Russian nobleman Michael Lazarev.

Keene was not happy to be placed in charge of Bloch's lackluster second string,

The Keene brothers had different personalities but shared an affinity for training racehorses; above, right, Ham might have been the better trainer, but Jack, far left, understood horses.

but he made the best of the banker's worst horses. In 1902 the horses Keene trained won more races than the first string and swept the country's most important contests.

His success raised the ire and suspicion of the Russians, who believed Keene was drugging his horses and sent gendarmerie to guard them before races. Keene's charges continued to win.

Keene enjoyed global success as a trainer; right, with Churchill Newcombe and W.V. Thraves.

After a brief visit to the United States, Keene returned to Russia as head trainer for the stable of Michael Lazarev, whose wife was the cousin of Tsar Nicholas II. Again, Keene was a success. His horses won 116 races in just over three months during the 1903 season. Accused again of drugging his horses, Keene left the country for good. Russian racing authorities barred Keene and other Americans, changing regulations to allow only Russian-born trainers to race there.

Five years later, in 1908, Keene was off to Japan, his trip funded by winnings from the racetrack. He was a gambler, even dabbling in bookmaking for a time, and luck was on his side in San Francisco when he and Roy Carruthers, who would later become Keeneland's first general manager, turned an eight dollar bet into more than $10,000 in winnings, an ample sum for an international adventure.

Arriving in Japan, Keene went racing and immediately liked what he saw — an opportunity to trounce the scrawny Chinese horses that ran there. He cabled his brother and asked Ham to send over several of their Thoroughbreds.

Ham shipped a trio of horses, Triumphant, Tonic, and Excitement. During the horses' quarantine, Keene trained them on a sandy beach near their quarters, and he later said it was the best facility he'd ever used. The three won sixteen races in one short meet and the dominance of the American-breds was said to have wrecked havoc on the Japanese wagering system.

As a trainer Keene was cagey, and quick to capitalize on opportunity. He quickly sized up Japanese racing as

sub par. In Russia, the lightweight shoes his horses wore, widely used in this country but not available there, made all the difference, he claimed.

In photos Keene appears steely, his jaw strong, his blue-eyed stare piercing. He was stubborn, determined, and eccentric, but under the prickly exterior, those who knew him well found a soft heart and a good deal of charm. "He could growl more than any man I ever knew, but under his skin he was a very kind and sympathetic person," said Brownie Leach, Keeneland's first publicity director.

Keene's friend John H. Clark, a public relations director for Keeneland and a bloodstock agent, called him "the most colorful personality I have encountered in any sport," a sweeping statement considering the dozens of sportsmen Clark knew.

Women found him attractive, and though there is a mention of an early, brief marriage, he never seemed to have a sustained romantic relationship.

Clark attributed it to heartbreak early in Keene's career, when he fell in love with

Keene, with William Pinkerton (right), was a familiar figure at major racing venues.

Jeanne Bowdre, a young woman from Memphis. Bowdre's parents did not approve of Keene because of his racetrack career. The relationship ended but Keene never forgot Bowdre, who had also loved horses and had asked Keene to name a filly for her.

A decade later, in 1919, he bred one worthy of her name and vowed never to part with Jeanne Bowdre or any of her fillies. Jeanne Bowdre produced ten winners for Keene, including Jean Valjean, Jean Lafitte, and Grand Slam. She lived out her life on the Keene farm, dying in the spring of 1943, just a few months before Keene.

In 1916, after a trip to England to buy bloodstock, Keene was back in the Bluegrass. Like other area horsemen, he raced at the Kentucky Association racetrack, built in the late 1820s on Lexington's northeast edge. Dissatisfied with the facilities there, Keene predicted the demise of the racetrack, which had been in decline after multiple owners and financial troubles. His prediction came true less than twenty years later.

Keene envisioned a better place to race, and his dreams, like their owner, were not idle. On the farm his family owned, a portion of the original Keen holdings, he began work on an alternative to the Kentucky Association track — a private club where he and his friends could train their horses and compete with one another.

He laid out a mile and one-sixteenth oval course on a rolling field at the edge of a ridge.

Keene's travels inspired his fondness for the low mortared stone walls that are a Keeneland signature.

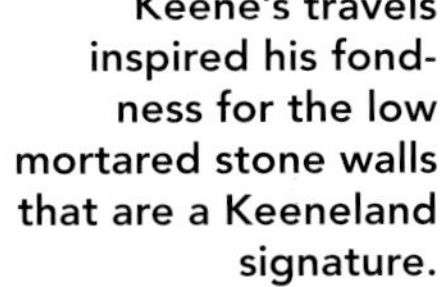

Keene had hoped to build a mile and one-eighth course, but the site proved too small without the addition of tons of fill dirt, an expensive venture.

His training complex needed an impressive entrance and so Keene hired local stonemasons to build a stone wall. As their guide, the workmen relied on sketches Keene had drawn while in England of a two-to-two pattern he admired there. It was a formation not seen in the Bluegrass, where rock walls were typically of the dry-stack style used in Ireland. By accident, the wall spurred the most massive undertaking of Keene's project: his "stone barn," a misnamed structure that was far more than a stable.

Keene incorporated handsome stone-work into the barns at his training center.

SET IN STONE

A demanding employer, Keene was especially hard to please when it came to stone construction. He had ordered his men to come up with two large cap stones to top the posts at Keeneland's entrance. They blasted away at quarries nearby, and time and again, their boss dismissed the rock they found as unsatisfactory. By the time they did find stones that suited, there was a huge pile of rejected limestone.

Keene did not want to waste the beautiful gray stone, and so he decided to build a "barn" next to his nascent race course — a barn that would house not only horses, but where he and his horse-racing pals could eat, sleep, drink, dance, and debate the issues of the industry and the day.

To be a man so particular, Keene wasn't much for planning. The design of his stone barn seemed mostly off-the-cuff. He personally stepped off the barn's dimensions; later, after reviewing plans for the barn that he'd asked an architect to draw up, Keene threw them in the fire. A man who "built by eye," as he liked to say, Keene could make little sense of the blueprints.

He was clear about what his barn would contain. There would be a dining hall for celebratory dinners, a ballroom for dances, comfortable living quarters for himself and for his friends, and a quarter-mile enclosed training track edged by stalls.

Over the next twenty years, work started and stopped on Keene's project. Not an overly wealthy man, he relied on winnings from the racetrack or proceeds from the sale of his bloodstock to get his pet project moving again. As his fortunes rose, there was a flurry of construction; when the funds ran out, the site went quiet.

When he and General Motors executive John Hertz, a horse owner and breeder, made money on a horse they owned in partnership, Keene asked Hertz to invest the proceeds in the stock market so the pair could buy an outstanding stallion. But when the fund grew to $200,000, Keene asked for his half — to use for his barn project.

At the time of its sale, Keene's dream project was unfinished. The new owners of the property incorporated stone into the major structures.

Keene was optimistic that the Keeneland Association would perpetuate his ideals.

The stone barn did slowly take shape. Keene would sometimes sit in a rocking chair, watching the workers, approving or disapproving as they laid the stone. As friend Henry McDaniel said, "Jack builds rock like he was Rockefeller."

Had Keene not been a Thoroughbred owner, breeder, and trainer, he might have been an architect, or, at the very least, a stone mason. "I went to work there to learn something about horses," said Charlie Kenney, a horseman who got his start with Keene. "I'm not certain what I learned about horses, but I learned helluva lot about rocks."

IMPRACTICAL GENIUS

Although most agreed patient, steady Ham was the better trainer in the family, Keene understood horses, a point that became clear as he designed his private racing facility.

He insisted that stalls at his farm be built with bars between them so the horses could see one another, contending that companionship would make for more contented horses, less likely to exhibit the nervous habits common to the breed. Others soon followed his lead, and the design became standard at Thoroughbred farms. Keene also designed a practice starting gate, which was applauded by other horsemen but was never patented.

Despite his obvious genius, Keene's inability to stick to a budget and his penchant for perfectionism would cause him and others problems throughout his life. One of his most colossal failures came in the early 1920s, when he headed a racetrack called Raceland near Ashland in northeastern Kentucky.

Racing at the time was concentrated in Lexington, Louisville, and northern Kentucky. Keene saw potential in northeastern Kentucky, where a well-placed racetrack could draw crowds from West Virginia and Ohio, as well as Kentucky. He found a site he deemed suitable and back to Lexington he came, rounding up influential friends in the horse business, convincing them to invest in his project.

Keene came away with $250,000, but he went overboard and over budget, spending $300,000 on barns and the track without managing to get a grandstand built. "He just honestly guessed the cost of building something — and missed by a country mile," said his friend Clark.

A smooth talker and salesman, Keene got another investor to throw in $100,000 and Raceland opened in July 1924.

Keene was sure the track and all its accoutrements, including sunken gardens and

Keene's "stable" became the foundation of the clubhouse and grandstand.

Keene's countenance grew crustier with age.

bridle paths, would appeal to the wealthy oil and gas tycoons in the region, but after four seasons Raceland closed, riddled by its debts.

The debacle at Raceland was a precursor to another economic undoing. As it did with most Americans, the Great Depression sent Jack Keene's finances into a free fall, and he realized he would never have the capital to finish his barn and racetrack project. He'd spent twenty years and more than $400,000, and still, his dream was less than half complete.

In 1935 he offered it to a group of men, many of whom he knew well, in the hopes they could do as a team what he as an individual had been unable to accomplish.

He was paid $130,000 and $10,000 in stock for his stone barn, his now-weedy racetrack, and 148 acres of land. After the sale was made, he summed up his dream:

"In planning and starting a racetrack at Keeneland Stud, it was my earnest hope to give the Bluegrass and Kentucky, my native state, a place where sportsmen and sportswomen might some day gather and enjoy Thoroughbred racing in its finest form. Changing conditions made it impossible to fulfill that desire. The Keeneland Association, I am sure, will carry out those ideals of perpetuating Thoroughbred racing as a means of improving the Thoroughbred and of establishing a place where racing is conducted as a sport."

On May 27, 1943, eight years after he sold his stone barn and racetrack to the men who did turn his dream into a reality, Jack Keene collapsed at the Fair Grounds racetrack in Detroit, Michigan, after watching his horses work. He died later that day, felled by a heart attack like his brother Ham, who died in 1927. The last of the men to carry the Keene name, he was buried in the family cemetery, behind the historic, ancestral home in which he was raised, bounded by a low stone wall, within a quarter mile of his great stone barn, now the clubhouse for Keeneland Race Course.

Over the years, as Keene's barn had taken form, many had called his project Keene's Castle; others had called it Keene's Folly. But when Keene was eulogized, Keeneland was called "his living monument."

KENTUCKY ASSOCIATION TRACK

Rena Baer

So integral is Keeneland to Lexington's identity that it feels like the city grew up around the racetrack rather than the other way around. But at seventy-five years of age, Keeneland is a relative youngster in Central Kentucky history. And, though it might be hard to imagine, Keeneland is not the city's longest-standing racetrack.

That distinction goes to the Kentucky Association track, which had an enviable run, opening in 1828 and enduring until 1933. The old track set the standards high for how racing should be conducted and established an expectation for great racing in the Bluegrass.

None of the racing records established at the Kentucky Association course still stand today. In fact, they all had been broken by 1936, but the reason had nothing to do with the caliber of the horses that ran there. The track was rough going; nothing like its smooth, well-kept successor, Keeneland.

"Those who remember the Kentucky Association track of yesteryear shake their heads as they watch the record-breakers of today fly over perfectly-made tracks and wonder what the same horses would have done over the Kentucky Association track a half century ago, or even in its later years," wrote "Brownie" Leach, the sports editor of the Lexington *Leader*, in the Keeneland 1936 souvenir book.

"Only horses with true hearts and tremendous courage had anything left when they came 'over the hill' off the back side of [the Kentucky Association track]. That hill was notorious. It broke the heart of many a Thoroughbred."

The Kentucky Association was formed in 1826 by several prominent locals in whose "veins flowed a sporting blood," according to *The Thoroughbred Record*. The mission of the group was to promote Thoroughbred racing and breeding, and the founders included

Many prominent citizens helped found the Kentucky Association track.

statesman Henry Clay, Jesse Bledsoe, Thomas F. Marshall, and Dr. Elisha Warfield, who bred Lexington, the most influential sire of the nineteenth century. Their vision was a far cry from Lexington's earliest racing, which consisted of horses running full blast down Main Street in the 1780s. Town trustees, fearing for the safety of the citizens, redirected these contests to the Commons.

Spectators would gather along High Street, which sat above the Commons, to view contests advertised in the *Kentucke Gazette*. In Newmarket fashion, the entrants would run the best two out of three heats at distances of three or four miles. Purses were paid from the one guinea subscription fee collected the previous day, often at a local tavern. The races were weight for age, with seven-year-old entrants carrying ten stone (140 pounds) and three-year-olds, "a feather" (five stones, or seventy pounds).

Lexington's wealthier pioneers, many of whom hailed from Virginia, appreciated fine bloodlines and had brought with them only their better stock to graze on the plentiful Kentucky bluegrass, upon which horses flourished. They bred some of these horses discerningly. From 1787 to 1805, the *Kentucke Gazette* ran many advertisements offering stallions for service in the Lexington area, suggesting payment in staples such as brick, "beef on foot," candles, gunpowder, tallow, salt, or brown sugar, and, of course, cash. Many of these stallions had been imported

Though Central Kentucky flourished as a Thoroughbred breeding center, its racetrack's fortunes waxed and waned over the years.

from England, and the advertisements included noble pedigrees printed at length and references to races run at Newmarket to substantiate the turf credentials.

In high demand were the offspring of Sir Archy, the son of Diomed, the first winner of England's Derby Stakes, who was imported to Virginia in 1798 at the age of twenty-one. "The Sir Archy blood is what Kentuckians seem to have been after," reported *The Thoroughbred Record* in 1921, "and soon there was more of it in Kentucky than in Virginia. Some six of Sir Archy's sons stood in the neighborhood of Lexington at one time, and there were mares there fit to mate with Diomed's grandsons."

Meanwhile, the first honest-to-goodness racetrack in the area had been constructed near Georgetown Pike, on what is now the Lexington Cemetery, in 1797. The course was known as the Williams track. That same year Kentucky horsemen organized for the

A competitive jockey colony characterized the Kentucky Association track.

first time by forming the Kentucky Jockey Club, whose rules and regulations also were adopted at courses outside the city.

The organization gave way to the Lexington Jockey Club in 1809, and racing continued until the War of 1812 brought things to a standstill. During the ensuing decade, racing was much less organized, and in 1823 the club finally faded from view. For the next three years racing migrated only to private tracks in the vicinity, including one at Ashland, the Henry Clay Estate.

On July 29, 1826, fifty of Kentucky's most prominent turfmen met at Mrs. Keene's inn to form the Kentucky Association for Improvement of the Breed of Horses. The objective set forth by the horsemen was "to improve the breed of horses by encouraging the sports of the turf." The men valued, above all, fairness and sought for the track to be "free from

A post and rail fence enclosed the track in its early years.

the vicious influence and dishonest methods that for a long time threatened to endanger the life of the sport in America," according to *The Thoroughbred Record*.

"There were no poolsellers or bookmakers; a third party to hold stakes in wagers — and they were often enormous — was considered unnecessary, and anything but a straightforward, upright course among owners, trainers and jockeys was unknown."

The association's first race meet started October 19, 1826, on the old Williams' track. The very first race consisted of four entrants running for a $300 purse, with Andrew Barnett's Diomed gelding, Sheriffe, sweeping the field in two straight heats. Regular race meets continued at the old track until the Kentucky Association track was constructed in 1828 on land purchased by John Postlethwaite and six other association trustees, all elected by association members, on what is now Aspendale Drive near Race and Fifth streets.

At the fall meet in 1830, the association continued to get organized, annexing a comprehensive list of rules and regulations that addressed items such as the number of judges, a jockey dress code, a scale of weights, and admission fees. The rules allowed that only members' horses could run for purses, providing there was satisfactory evidence of the horse's age and that the subscription fee had been paid. Regulations prohibited two jockeys from the same stable or two horses trained by the same stable to run in the same race. The rules also addressed collusion, specified as an agreement of horsemen not to oppose each other or to conspire to defeat another. "In either case upon satisfactory evidence, produced before the Judges, the purse shall be awarded to the next best nag, and the person so offending shall never again be permitted to

start a horse on this course," the rules stated.

The regulations prohibited gambling on the grounds, but this did not include betting the races. Wagers were often huge, but there were no pools sold in the early days nor were there any bookmakers in the track's earlier years. Owners were expected to wager with all comers, accepting their money and then settling after the heat or the race.

The track also was not immune to outside racing forces, conforming in 1834 to the scale of weights established by the Central Course of Maryland. A motion also was adopted to have the racing secretary publish a bulletin of the races every morning during the spring and fall meets that described the horses and the riders' dress. In addition, the track grounds were expanded that year to sixty-five acres. An early frequenter of the track later described it in *History of Lexington*, published in 1872:

"We can recollect when nothing but an old post and rail fence inclosed (sic) the track; the judges' stand stood at the cow-pens, and the grand stand was an old rickety building, with high steps, which stood on top of the hill in the center of the course."

The course purportedly was fenced in 1835, the same year Sarah Miller, Jim Allen, and Grayfoot met in a much celebrated sixteen-mile race. Three years later, Lexington crowds thrilled to the debut of Gray Eagle, a three-year-old son of Woodpecker out of

Racegoers sported their finest attire for a day at the track.

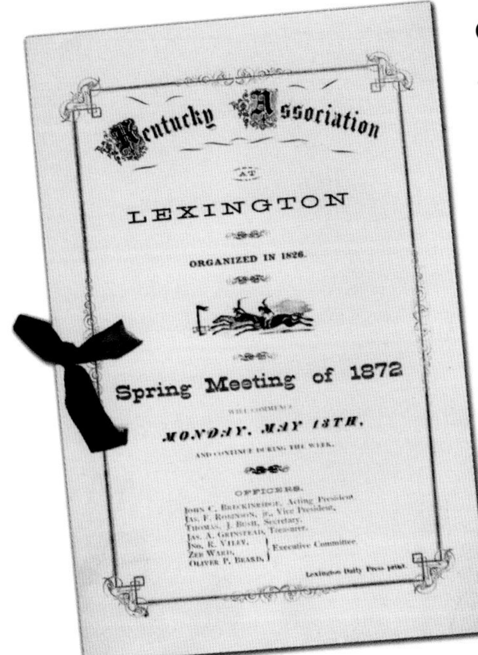

Celebrated jockey Isaac Murphy won his first race at the track.

Ophelia. The beautiful gray with a flowing silver mane and tail soon became a Kentucky idol and champion. A year later he faced off in Louisville against the renowned Wagner, losing to the offspring of Sir Charles out of Maria West in front of "old and young — rich and poor — grave and gay — in short everybody that could spare the time and raise the means was there," according to an account given by *The Sporting Times'* William T. Porter.

The year 1840 took on significance at the Lexington track as an unprecedented nine stallions started for a great three-mile heat race, in which Blacknose beat his competitors, setting an American record of 5:40 in the first heat. The following year, Jim Bell set a national record of 1:46 for the mile, which stood for many years.

The first Phoenix Hotel Stakes was run in 1831. Named for the landmark Phoenix Hotel that helped Lexington become known as "the Athens of the West," the Phoenix Stakes went through several title changes before returning to the original. Considered the oldest stakes race in the country, the Phoenix Stakes, as well as a few others initiated by the Kentucky Association, is still run today at Keeneland, outliving its namesake, which was demolished in 1982.

The Great Produce Stakes for three-year-olds was inaugurated as well during this time in 1843 and had the distinction of becoming the most valuable race ever run in Kentucky in the early days. The race once had seventy-two subscribers at $500 each, $100 forfeit, with a $500 gold cup added. Ruffin, by Hedgford, out of Duchess of Marlborough, by Sir Archy was the winner.

It was also at the Lexington track that the tremendous Lexington, who was named Darley at birth for his likeness to John Sartorious' painting of the Darley Arabian, made his debut on May 23, 1853, in the Association Stakes, formerly the Phoenix Hotel Stakes (the hotel had tired of paying $100 toward the winning plate). Lexington was bred by esteemed association founder Warfield, who had liked the spot chosen for the track so much that he bought 123 adjacent acres and built a mansion, calling his homestead The Meadows.

In his debut, on a track knee deep in mud, Lexington was part of an edgy group that bolted before the start. Despite covering two miles before the official break, he led the field in the mile-long heat, from the fall of the flag to the finish. He completed the second heat in the same commanding fashion, bewitching everyone who was watching and leading owners to reach into their pockets to make offers to buy him.

It was only the beginning for the great runner, who went on to become the property of Richard Ten Broeck and his syndicate, winning six of seven starts to become the third-leading money earner of his time before he began to lose his sight. Rapidly going blind, he was bought by R.A. Alexander as a sire for $15,000, an incredible price for the times, but a bargain as he became the nation's leading sire sixteen times.

During the Civil War racing continued at every available opportunity, though many breeders and owners sent their steeds out of state for safekeeping as troops began raiding farms for cavalry stock. Some of the most promising of Lexington's first progeny were used as cavalry mounts and were killed in battle.

Following the Civil War, the Kentucky Association track was regraded in 1872 and widened from forty feet to seventy feet. In addition a new wooden grandstand, with a lower story built of brick, and a new octagonal judges' stand were built, along with eleven barns that could house seventy-five horses. George W. Ranck described it as "one of the handsomest [tracks] in the United States" in his 1872 book, *History of Lexington*.

A new wooden grandstand was among the improvements after the Civil War.

Racing spent the next several years growing in popularity, attracting many new owners and breeders, and leading off an era of exceptional horses such as Aristides, Ten Broeck, Mollie McCarty, Domino, and many other brilliant runners. It also was an era that introduced the exceptional African American jockey Isaac Burns Murphy, who earned his first win, at the Lexington track, on September 16, 1876.

"It was the period during which the clubhouse was constructed," wrote Leach. "It was marked by burgoo feasts at the track prior to the opening of the race meetings, of champagne parties given at the clubhouse each year by the winning owner of the Phoenix Hotel Stakes. It was the period when bookmakers made their debut, when pools were sold at the Phoenix Hotel on the eve of the race.

"The period saw the introduction of dash races. It was marked by annual stallion shows in Lexington during the race meeting. It was during this period that horses were raced for the fun of racing, when citizens of different counties disregarded breeding, form and everything else as they rallied in patriotic support to back the horse bred in their community with no regard for opposition."

The most memorable race in the track's history took place in 1876 during its golden anniversary celebration. Price McGrath's Aristides, a grandson of Lexington who had a year earlier won the very first Kentucky Derby, was once again taking on Richard Harper's mighty Ten Broeck from Woodford County in a two and five-eighths mile race. All the other entrants had scratched for sundry reasons.

"The beauty and chivalry of the fair Bluegrass section was gathered there to witness the race," wrote John H. Davis in *The American Turf*. "There were bookmakers in plenty on the ground ready to take the money of those who desired to wager. But Price McGrath mounted a box and shouted to the people:

" 'Come on if you want to bet against my horse. I will take all your money and give you the same odds the bookies offer. You will lose what you bet anyhow. You might as well give it to a neighbor whom you all know. Come on; don't be afraid. I am here ready for business. You know me. You know I can pay and that I will do it. Give me your money. I need it.' "

Soon the great big pockets of his long linen duster were bulging with money, including

At one time the Kentucky Association track was considered among the most handsome in the country.

Kentucky's racetracks were the first to adopt pari-mutel betting.

several thousand dollars of his own. McGrath was taking it in with both hands, depending on the honor of each man to keep his own account. He continued until the first tap of the bell, announcing it was time for the horses to warm up.

Aristides was ridden by the noted Bobby Swim while Ten Broeck had the famous African American jockey Billy Walker in the saddle. The crowd rushed to the rail to see the ensuing battle between the powerhouses. Ten Broeck kept the lead coming off the backside hill, but as Swim loosened his hold on the little brown McGrath horse, he immediately went after his Woodford County-bred neighbor.

"Into the stretch they turned, jockeys and horses rushing down on a screaming mass of humans. Slowly but surely the first Derby winner was pulling away. Ten Broeck could not match his strides and fell back to finish forty yards behind the winner in 3:45½. Woodford County was bankrupt. Its residents had bet their last dollar, their last nickel on their champion," wrote Davis.

Three years later the Ashland Oaks was inaugurated. From the track's inception, Henry Clay had been an active officer in the association, and in 1879 the race for three-year-old fillies at one mile was created and named in honor of the statesman's estate. The race, now known as the Ashland Stakes, is still run today, at Keeneland, though the distance has been stretched to a mile and a sixteenth. From its early years to the present, its winners have been tried and tested, many going on to greater racing and broodmare careers.

The May 7, 1898, Ashland Oaks, when Major Barak G. Thomas' Jewel Ban beat Brown Princess and Retrieve at the finish line, took the honor of being one of the most exciting races ever run at the Kentucky Association track. According to the 1936 Keeneland souvenir book, a handkerchief could have covered the noses of the first three finishers:

"Into the stretch came this trio matching nostrils and their respective riders frantic in their efforts to pull away. Down the straightaway the three horses matched stride for stride while a frenzied crowd rushed to the rail to see the finish.

"Ten feet from the wire Jockey Cooper shoved Jewel Ban's nose in front. Brown Princess reached out in an effort to match it, but barely poked her nose in front of the favored Retrieve. The other starters were forgotten."

The track had been sold in 1890 to National Realty Company, a group of investors, which had franchised the track to the New Kentucky Association, continuing the meets up until 1898. The Panic of 1893 had dealt a serious financial blow to the track, and the new owners were having difficulty attracting horses. The 1896 Ashland Oaks had been described as "a farce" by the New York Times after it only drew two entries. In 1899 the track was closed down and hemp was grown in the infield for two years while a few horses trained there. In 1903 the track was leased to W.C. Lyne and Clark Farrish for training.

In 1904 Captain S.S. Brown, a coal operator, Pittsburg hotel proprietor, and turf magnate, purchased the property and made many improvements. Racing resumed the following May, starting the final chapters in the track's long history.

Pari-mutuel betting came along in 1906, legally replacing bookmakers at the Lexington track in 1908. This form of betting came from French pools (known as Paris mutuels, hence the name pari-mutuel). In 1908 the state ruled valid pari-mutuel wagering in an

An early souvenir from the Kentucky Association track.

Champagne flowed in the clubhouse after major stakes races.

enclosure of a racetrack but condemned handbooks in pool rooms without the enclosure of a racetrack.

Meanwhile, in the latter part of 1906, the track had been bought back by a group of Kentucky horsemen that included Senator Johnson M. Camden, Charles F. Grainer, Matt Winn, Charles F. Price, E.R. Bradley, Hal Petit Headley, whose son would help found Keeneland three decades later, and several other Lexington residents. These men reorganized the Kentucky Association and the first meet under this new leadership was held in May 1907.

In 1910 the track added a new race to its autumn program, the Breeders' Futurity, which never failed to bring together a fine field of two-year-olds. It became the autumn meet's feature event, and its winner always ranked high when the betting commission drew up its future odds on the Kentucky Derby. The race was later moved to Old Latonia when Lexington abandoned its fall races in 1930. It is now a prestigious Keeneland stakes race for two-year-olds in the fall.

The Blue Grass Stakes, Keeneland's signature spring race and an important prep for the Kentucky Derby, got its start in 1911 and was run twelve times from its inception until 1926. Its winner usually became the horse to root for "in the West" when the Derby followed later in the spring. However, only Bubbling Over managed to turn that double, in 1926, after he ran off from his field and merely galloped home in the Blue Grass Stakes.

A 1928 button tag qualified the bearer for free admission.

The track had been sold once again, in 1918, this time to the Kentucky Jockey Club, which had then sold it to one hundred Lexingtonians who had incorporated under the name Kentucky Association. S.S. Combs was selected as president and Thomas C. Bradley as vice president and manager.

On January 27, 1921, a massive crowd gathered at the track to watch the legendary Man o' War gallop under silks before he retired to Hinata Farm in Lexington. It was a special occasion, given the great racehorse had never run in Kentucky.

The Kentucky Association track closed for good in 1933 due to inept management, a series of fires, and no room to grow in its downtown Lexington location. The government bought the property for $1,000 an acre (later building public housing on the land), with a physical property sale providing an additional $8,411, bringing bondholders a total $75,446 minus debt amounting to $13,391.

Hal Price Headley expressed the hope that bondholders would reinvest the money in Keeneland. Many took him up on what proved to be a very wise move. After seventy-five years, Keeneland has remained stalwart and synonymous with the Bluegrass, much of it by remaining loyal to its roots and to the mission of the Kentucky Association.

BUILDING ON A SOLID FOUNDATION

Vickie Mitchell

The fall day was fair; the racetrack, fast. A newspaperman on the scene for Keeneland's opening day sized up the fashionable crowd and proclaimed it "a miniature Kentucky Derby assemblage," attended by "the kings and queens of society and the Napoleons of finance and business."

At seven minutes before 2 p.m. on October 15, 1936, a spotted pony carrying outrider Joe Moran stepped onto the plowed dirt and led eight prancing Thoroughbreds in the first-ever post parade at Keeneland Race Course. A hush fell over the crowd of 8,000 that spilled from the new 2,500 seat grandstand and across the lawn, as they anticipated the return of racing to Lexington.

It took thirteen months to transform Jack Keene's training center into a model racetrack.

In little more than thirteen months, John Oliver "Jack" Keene's private track had been turned into what its creators hoped would be "a model racetrack," revered not only for its gracious grounds but for its unorthodox organization, a nonprofit structure designed to improve the sport and the community rather than line its founders' pockets with profits.

As Royal Raiment, a two-year-old gray filly owned by John Hay Whitney, crossed the finish line in the six-furlong contest and became Keeneland's inaugural winner, all in attendance felt victorious, with or without a winning ticket in hand.

In little more than thirteen months, John Oliver "Jack" Keene's private track had been turned into what its creators hoped would be "a model racetrack," revered not only for its gracious grounds but for its unorthodox organization, a nonprofit structure designed to improve the sport and the community rather than line its founders' pockets with profits.

Above, Royal Raiment became Keeneland's first winner; below, Major Louie A. Beard, left, and Hal Price Headley were a formidable duo.

TENUOUS START

For Keeneland president Hal Price Headley and Major Louie A. Beard, chief fundraiser for the new track, the triumph was tempered by trepidation. The pair, more than anyone else present, realized Keeneland's financial footing was far from solid — the smallest of stumbles or the tiniest of missteps could undo the pretty little racetrack.

As each of the first day's races ended, Headley fidgeted in a wooden chair in his clubhouse box, scrutinizing the numbers on the track's state-of-the-art electronic tote board, the totalizator. He did his math, calculating whether the track could cover the winning bets and reopen the next day.

His concern went unnoticed by the crowd. Writer Neville Dunn reported that the first day's program "went off smooth

as silk." The last race started thirty minutes behind schedule, only because the crowds overwhelmed the betting windows.

When the nine-day meet ended, Keeneland had scraped by, losing just $3.47 in its first year. Lexington, a town of 46,000, had supported racing's comeback, as the new track posted a meet attendance of 25,337.

And even with 15 million Americans out of work, those fans had taken a gamble or two, betting $534,497 in nine days of racing. Horse owners trotted away with $53,500 in purses.

Enthusiasm for Keeneland would not diminish. A year later the track would end its second year up $8,286; a year after that, in 1938, it would make good on one of the promises of its prospectus and make its first gift to charity, presenting the Lexington Community Chest with $500.

UNCONVENTIONAL TRACK

When the Kentucky Association racetrack closed in 1933, Lexington was without a racetrack for the first time in 107 years. But even before the track's demise, horsemen and town leaders had talked of building another. The Kentucky Association track, a storied place whose founders included statesman Henry Clay, had had its day, and inattentive and inconsistent management, coupled with poor upkeep and the city's encroachment on its urban site, had made it "an unlovely affair," according to the Keeneland prospectus.

Headley, considered one of the most influential Thoroughbred owners and breeders of his generation, and others believed Lexington's next racetrack should be in the country where it could showcase the rolling Bluegrass countryside.

Left, Headley lent mules from his farm to break ground for the track; the grandstand takes shape.

Constructing a racetrack during the
Great Depression took a leap of faith.
Note the ponds in the infield: They
were drained and filled soon after
opening due to the blinding glare
they caused with the afternoon sun.

KEENELAND EDITION THE LEXINGTON HERALD KEENELAND EDITION

THEY'RE OFF! AT KEENELAND

TO KEEP AFLAME THE SPIRIT OF TRUE SPORTSMANSHIP

THE FINEST OF THOROUGHBREDS

Nine Days of Racing at Its Best

October 15th to 24th

BE THERE THURSDAY FOR THE OPENING BUGLE

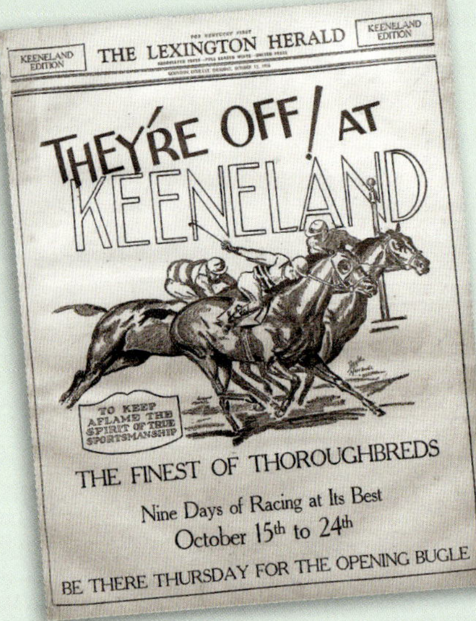

A committee of ten men, led by Beard, began the search for a new site. From twenty potential locations, they pared the list to five, with Jack Keene's private racetrack at Keeneland Stud topping the list.

The committee favored Keeneland for several reasons. For one, Keene was willing to part with 148 acres and all the improvements he'd made for a price far less than the property's value. There was a dependable spring on site, a major consideration in the days before city water lines stretched out to the countryside.

And finally, all the work Keene had done — from his racecourse and 100,000-gallon water tower to his by-now locally famous stone barn — would give the new racetrack a running start.

And so the Keeneland Association was formed, led by a board of twenty-one directors. There were, of course, horse owners and breeders among them but also a banker, a hotelier, a doctor, and a judge. Those who had never owned, raced, or bred a horse were chosen for just that reason — they were to represent other aspects of the community.

From the outset, it was clear Keeneland would not be a conventional racetrack. The men who conceived it believed the track should be a community project, a nonprofit venture in which proceeds would be plowed back into better purses for horsemen and improvements to the facilities, with any remaining profits to be donated to local charities.

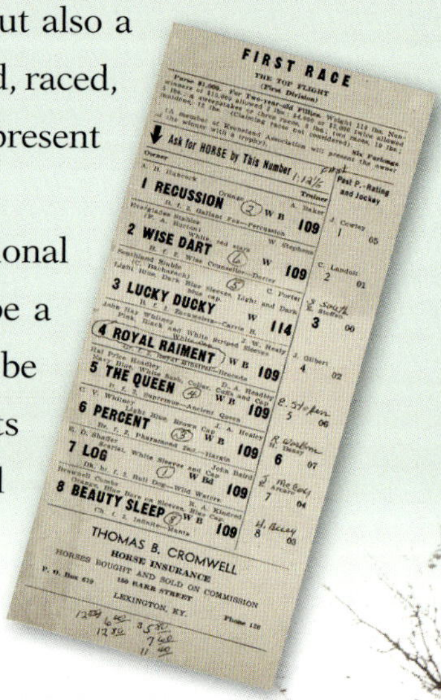
FIRST RACE

THE TOP FLIGHT

(First Division)

Ask for HORSE by This Number

1 RECUSSION W B 109

2 WISE DART W 109

3 LUCKY DUCKY W 114

4 ROYAL RAIMENT W B 109

5 THE QUEEN W B 109

6 PERCENT W B 109

7 LOG W Bd 109

8 BEAUTY SLEEP W B 109

THOMAS B. CROMWELL

HORSE INSURANCE

HORSES BOUGHT AND SOLD ON COMMISSION

LEXINGTON, KY.

The program for the opening meet in 1936 shows the first race, right, on October 15.

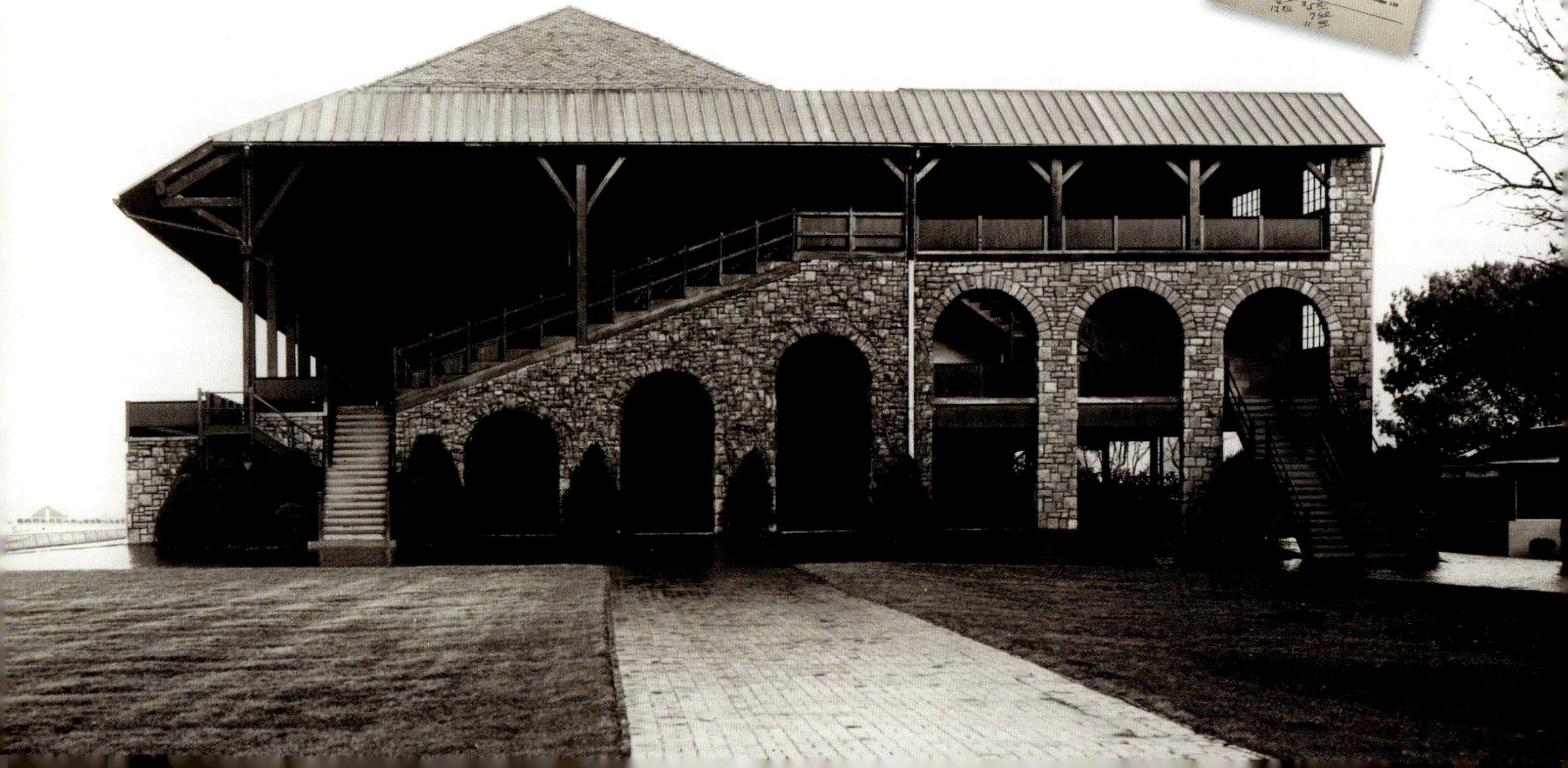

The unusual concept, the founders hoped, would make for a racetrack immune to economic ills. Money to build it would also come from the community, through the sale of stock — stock that would never pay dividends.

In its prospectus, the track was described as "a model racetrack dedicated solely to the perpetuation and improvement of the sport and specifically committed never to seek profits, except insofar as it may be necessary to pay interest upon money used."

It would differ from the Kentucky Association track in a number of ways. There, many patrons paid no admission. At Keeneland there would be "no free passes." Admission for ladies would be fifty cents; for men the charge would be one dollar.

There would also be few paid staff; many committee members and board members would volunteer as stewards and judges. No officer or director would ever be paid.

When Headley, Beard, and other leaders explained their plan to 200 citizens in the spring of 1935 at the Lafayette Hotel, there were doubters who said, "Keeneland will never make it. It's way out in the country with no public transportation. No free passes. No public address system. It gets its water from Manchester Spring, which it sure as hell will pump dry."

Beard worked behind the scenes to raise money to build Keeneland.

But others, familiar with the determined man at the helm, countered the negative claims. "Don't underestimate Price Headley. He can flip a silver dollar into the air and have it come down gold."

EFFECTIVE TEAM

Like many good friends, Headley and Beard were nothing alike, and it was their differences that made them a powerful pair. They and a young man named William T. Bishop were the forces behind Keeneland's successful opening.

Headley, a Lexington native, was a Princeton man who had returned to his family's farm after college to run his family's tobacco warehouse business and manage his Beaumont Farm, where he raised Thoroughbreds and tobacco.

A dizzyingly busy man, Headley could be abrasive and abrupt, and those who weren't well acquainted with his steamrolling style often deemed him rude.

Well-to-do, but also well respected, Headley had worked hard for what he had. John H. Clark, a bloodstock agent and public relations director for Keeneland, once said, "Hal Price Headley did the work and thinking and planning of five men."

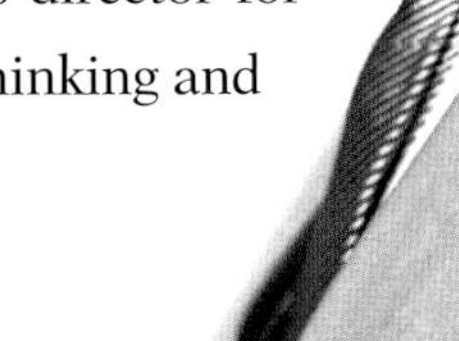

Beard was the quieter and gentler of the pair. Born in Texas, he graduated from West Point and later served under General George S. Patton. A champion polo player and a horseman, Beard had left the military in 1925 to manage the Lexington Thoroughbred farms owned by the Whitney family, including Greentree and the C.V. Whitney farm.

The drastic differences in their personalities were summed up by trainer Tom B. Young. "Price is trying to make a horseman out of Louie, and Louie is trying to make a gentleman out of Price — and they are both failing."

Their roles in the Keeneland project suited them. Accustomed to driving his workers hard on the farm, Headley had no problem taking the helm at Keeneland, firing off orders, making fast decisions, and setting a breakneck work pace. The master of Beaumont Farm had become the master of Keeneland and the intensity of his involvement was lost on no one. As Keene Daingerfield, a Kentucky racing steward, said, "every brick and stone at Keeneland has a drop of Price Headley's blood on it."

In the background, Beard made his calls to the genteel mansions and plush offices of the Thoroughbred owners and others, convincing them to provide their financial support.

In short, their jobs boiled down to this, as Bishop so succinctly put it: "Major Beard raised the money; Price Headley spent it wisely."

COUNTING PENNIES

In just five weeks, Beard's fund raising had scraped together a little more than $250,000, enough to buy and start work on the racetrack. The group would eventually raise nearly another $100,000; $55,000 from selling lifetime clubhouse memberships at $500 each, Beard's innovative idea.

To get the job done with what little money was on hand required penny pinching. Bishop was the only paid full-time employee, hired at $1,800 a year; the rest of the staff was seasonal. Headley brought men and mules from his farm to work at Keeneland.

To economize further, Headley headed to the dispersal of the Kentucky Association track, where he bought the framing and roofing for five barns and 1,500 grandstand seats at fifty cents apiece.

His most brilliant acquisition was a cast-iron post, more than 100 years old. The letters KA, for the Kentucky Association, were

In short, their jobs boiled down to this, as Bishop so succinctly put it: "Major Beard raised the money; Price Headley spent it wisely."

emblazoned upon it. "Get that too," Headley told his men. "I don't care how many men it takes to get it loaded." He had a plan for the post and its two-letter monogram. It would become the entrance marker for the Keeneland Association's new racecourse.

LITTLE MORE THAN A PLOWED PATH

Arriving at the site of the new race track in September 1936, Bishop, or "Bish" as he became known, had no inkling of the long workdays ahead for him.

Bishop was twenty-two, a recent graduate of the University of Kentucky. He had approached Headley about a job at Keeneland on the advice of his friend, sports writer Joe Estes, who thought racetrack management a field with excellent potential for a business administration major such as Bishop. Estes was correct. Bishop eventually became Keeneland's general manager; he held the position for thirty-six years.

Although Bishop had been to a racetrack only once, he was a quick study and convinced the skeptical Headley he could do the job.

Bishop became Keeneland's first paid employee and enjoyed a long tenure at the track.

Given its beauty today, it is hard to imagine Keeneland as shabby, and yet, that's what Bishop and others found in the fall of 1935.

Keene's track, roughly laid out four years earlier, was little more than a plowed path in a field. Weeds poked up through the broken soil with enthusiasm. Keene's tobacco crop grew in the infield; a big barn was nearby to house it.

His stone barn stood like a medieval fortress, its lines harsh and square. A sinkhole had swallowed much of the earth where a grandstand would be built; the quarter-mile enclosed training track was half finished.

What Keene had left was definitely rough, but with the right polish it had potential. His barn would be transformed into the racetrack's clubhouse. It's great room, warmed by a massive fireplace large enough for logs six feet long and three feet wide, would become the clubhouse's main entry. The beamed ceilings topped out at twenty feet and a staircase led to balconies branching off to two wings, both of which offered spaces that would become dining rooms for guests and offices for staff. Keene had dreamed big and his barn's forty-four rooms, twenty-car garage, and stable for a dozen racehorses would all find new purposes in Keeneland's new plans.

Even Keene's indoor training track, an idea inspired by the success he'd seen come

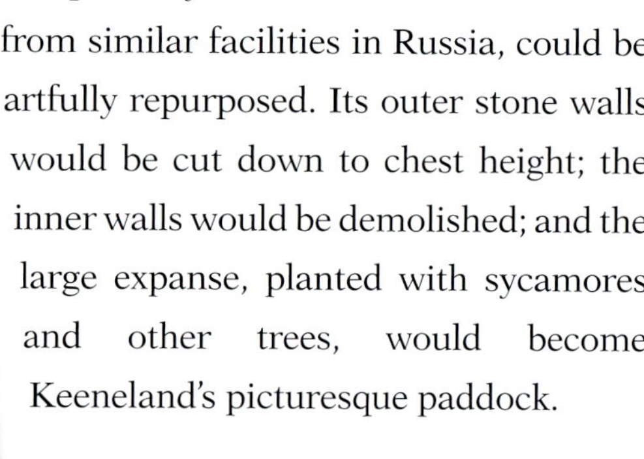

from similar facilities in Russia, could be artfully repurposed. Its outer stone walls would be cut down to chest height; the inner walls would be demolished; and the large expanse, planted with sycamores and other trees, would become Keeneland's picturesque paddock.

AMBITIOUS SCHEDULE

The Keeneland founders were an ambitious and optimistic bunch. They took ownership of Keene's property in September and were convinced they would open their new racetrack the following April.

The work schedule was rigorous. When architect Robert McMeekin told Beard he needed time off to go on his honeymoon, the quick retort was, "The hell you do. You have to finish this clubhouse."

It was McMeekin, already gaining a reputation in Lexington for the handsome homes

The prospectus used to sell shares in Keeneland extolled Central Kentucky's racing heritage.

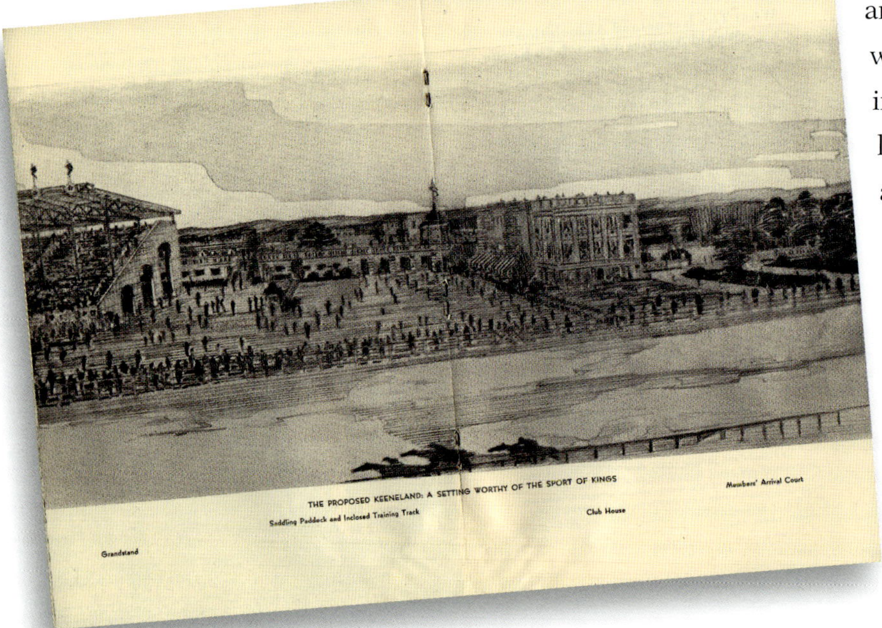

Hal Price Headley presents the trophy for the 1936 Keene Handicap to Brownell Combs; high quality and intricate designs make Keeneland trophies dearly prized.

he was building of stone, who softened the hard lines of Keene's castle with gabled roofs, a wooden porch, and a front portico. He also designed the 2,500-seat grandstand, built of wood as Beard had demanded. "I'm tired of backing my ass up against a piece of steel on a cold day and I want an all wood grandstand," Beard told McMeekin.

But even with Bishop and his crews working from 6 a.m. to 6 p.m., seven days a week, with days off only for Thanksgiving and Christmas, the deadline became an unreachable one as an unusually bitter winter slowed work.

As with any building project, there were problems and the condition of Keene's racetrack was a big one. Although the track was generously wide, it was nowhere near level. Tons of dirt had to be scraped, shifted, and hauled to iron it out.

There was also the issue of repurposing Keene's plans. Much of what Keene had built had to be dismantled, and much of the demolition was done as he watched.

As part of the sale, he had been granted quarters in the large stone edifice (and a lifetime membership to the Keeneland clubhouse). He had also kept the other half of his family farm, next to Keeneland, where he would eventually build another barn and home, both of stone, of course.

Just as they do to-day, early fans lined the perimeter of the saddling area.

As Bishop and his crews feverishly worked to ready Keeneland for opening, Keene observed, much as he had for the past twenty years when he owned the place. He didn't much care for what he saw, as crews dynamited stone pillars that seemed to have no purpose and demolished the interior walls of his indoor training track.

Bishop remembered, "He stood up there under the old clubhouse roof and watched my men who were at work out there and, with solid tears in his eyes, the old man really was crying over the fact that we were destroying what he had built in there and what he had planned."

EXCITEMENT BUILDS

Race meets at the Kentucky Association track had long caused celebration in Lexington. There were burgoo feasts and champagne toasts. Ladies spent weeks planning pre- and post-race soirees.

But when the Kentucky Association track, the nation's longest operating racetrack at the time, shut down for good in 1933, the social swirl it inspired came to a halt.

And so it was not surprising that with Keeneland's opening, Lexingtonians were once again ready for a party or two.

The days before and during the first meet were filled with luncheons, receptions, and dinners.

The Headleys entertained at their Beaumont Farm. A.B. Gay, the track's first vice president, invited forty friends to a luncheon at the new clubhouse. Another Keeneland founder, Horatio Mason, was toasted by his guests from New York, New Orleans, and Washington, D.C., at a country club gathering he hosted. A Junior League dance at the Lexington Country Club was considered one of the highlights of the new racing-inspired social season. An estimated 15,000 people poured through Keeneland's gates the Sunday before the race meet for a public open house.

Guest lists went beyond locals. At the Lafayette Hotel, guests checked in from New York, New Orleans, Los Angeles, Miami Beach, Chicago, and Detroit.

Main Street, with the hope that racing's return would invigorate sales in the midst of the Depression, stocked merchandise for race goers. At Kaufman's, a double-breasted Glen plaid suit with deep-notched wide lapels could be had for $35; at Angelucci and Ringo, striped silk ties were offered in the colors of thirty racing stables for $1.50 each.

On opening day, traffic was unprecedented on Versailles Pike, as 8,000 people piled into their cars to reach a racetrack unserved by public transportation. One Versailles

Road resident counted 154 cars pass his house in a nine-minute span, a rate that would equal 1,020 cars an hour. For those without a car, Deluxe Cab offered "the quick way to Keeneland," a cab ride of 25 cents for up to three passengers.

Left, spectators watch as horses prepare to enter the paddock; above, the clubhouse crowd observes the field in the post parade.

JOB WELL DONE

In a letter, Beard once described Keeneland as "the result of an original small idea which Price and I with many others kicked around, and added to here and there, until it has grown into its present form."

Keeneland's form reflects the time, place, and people that created it.

It copied little from its peers: Churchill Downs and its clapboard and spires; Saratoga and its country fair charm; Santa Anita and its sleek, modern lines.

Keeneland seemed to have stepped from the nineteenth century, and in some ways, it preferred to operate in the old ways. At Beard's insistence, with Headley in agreement, there was no public address system. The founders thought it important for race goers to learn the sport and how to follow the race, without the shrill call of an announcer.

In the early days, mules and horses pulled plows and the starting gate; Headley and Beard thought tractors left hard spots in the dirt.

The clubhouse, as handsome as McMeekin's tweaks had made it, was still unorthodox, sitting at the top of the stretch instead of near the first turn, facing the west and the wind. It made sense in Keene's plan — he had thought he and his friends would race their horses in the morning, with the sun warming their backs.

But it was in part because of those quirks that Keeneland quickly became a point of local pride, a place to be reminded of the beauty and bounty of the Bluegrass.

It was a job well done.

KEENELAND ...
AND THEY'RE OFF!

MICHELE MACDONALD

F ew plans, even those crafted by the most farsighted men and women, spring to life just as imagined, much less survive the tides of nearly eight decades. That Keeneland Race Course has endured and even superseded the idealistic vision that led to its opening in 1936 is a tribute to those who envisioned a natural showcase for the Thoroughbred and to those who have continued to make this dream a reality.

Keeneland was never intended to be just another racetrack. And it never has been.

"We want a place where those who love horses can come and picnic with us and thrill to the sport of the Bluegrass. We are not running a race plant to hear the click of the mutuel machines," declared Keeneland's first president, Hal Price Headley. "We want them to come out here to enjoy God's sunshine, the fresh air, and to watch horses race."

Champion Myrtle-wood graced the opening program; the 1942 Ashland trophy presentation with Eddie Arcaro

Not only have horses been running at Keeneland since the track was constructed on the foundation of a unique racing complex begun by John Oliver "Jack" Keene on his family's farmland, a vivid parade of America's best racehorses has flashed across this bucolic horizon.

From the very first program that featured champion sprinter and handicap female Myrtlewood — who achieved more fame as an extraordinary broodmare from whom descended Triple Crown winner Seattle Slew and leading sire Mr. Prospector — great horses have left their hoofprints on the Keeneland grounds. They were, of course, accompanied by the footsteps of racing's greatest human competitors. Among the trainers represented by runners in Keeneland's very first race was future Racing Hall of Famer Woodford C. "Woody" Stephens, the Kentucky native who five decades later would set a remarkable record by saddling five consecutive winners of the Belmont Stakes.

Every decade has unfurled its own array of legends at Keeneland, with some of the more recent including Azeri, who earned the gold Eclipse Award as 2002 Horse of the Year; Street Sense, champion juvenile and winner of the 2007 Kentucky Derby; and Rachel Alexandra, the superstar of 2009 who, after winning at Keeneland as a juvenile, defeated America's best males in three grade I races topped by the Preakness Stakes.

In fact, so many champions have trod across Keeneland over time that track officials do not even have a count of them. Some, such as Racing Hall of Fame geldings John Henry and Forego, who each earned two Horse of the Year titles, never gained a win at Keeneland, where the sport is quite possibly more competitive than anywhere in North America.

Inset, early Keeneland postcard; the site plan from the original prospectus

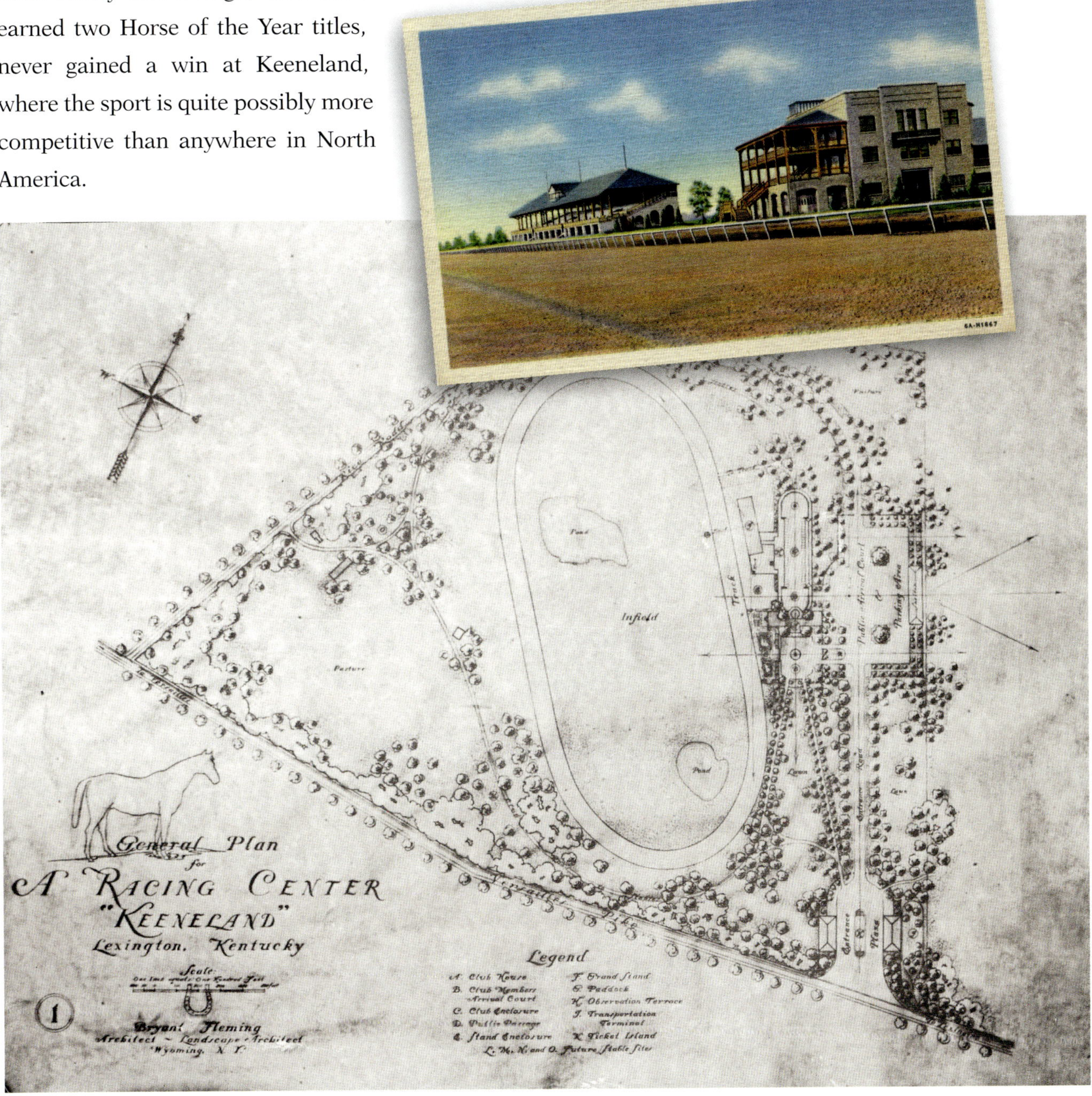

Workers prepare to install the tote board; below, Hal Price Headley bundles up on a cool day.

When the Keeneland Association was founded in 1935 following the demise two years earlier of the Kentucky Association's track at the end of Lexington's Fifth Street, where racing had been conducted since 1828, high standards were made the rule. From the beginning, Keeneland was designed to be "America's model race course," as a special souvenir magazine proclaimed in a headline, and "a national track, a place where Thoroughbred racing will be really perpetuated for sport and for the value of races as tests for breeding stock."

Based initially on 148 acres, the complex was hewn from Keene's original 1 1/16-mile track and a large building made of stone quarried on the property. Keene already had spent approximately $400,000 on what he dreamed would be a living monument to horse racing and thus the initial Keeneland facilities could be completed for only an additional $300,000, an opportunity founders determined was unmatched.

A partially completed enclosed training track, which Keene had designed as part of the racing center he could not complete after reverses in the Great Depression, was converted into the saddling paddock.

On October 15, 1936, Keeneland opened with about 8,000 fans on hand to witness seven races worth a total of $7,380 and to wager with the first totalizator equipment in Kentucky — just the first of many initiatives Keeneland would pioneer. Keene took out an advertisement thanking the association for "the distinct honor" of carrying on with his family's name as well as fulfilling his "earnest hope" to present "Thoroughbred racing in its finest form" on the land.

Even in their most optimistic musings, however, neither Keene nor the founders of Keeneland probably could have foreseen what ensued in the succeeding years.

TRANSFORMING GOALS TO GREATNESS

From the earliest moments, the directors of Keeneland determined a course they wanted to follow and they have not veered from that path. Among the earliest goals was the development of races, including stakes, for fillies and mares to prove their worth as breeding stock; an emphasis on preparatory events, such as the Blue Grass Stakes,

Royal Raiment, left, won Keeneland's first race; Double-dogdare won major fily races

during the spring meets for the classics, most notably the Kentucky Derby in nearby Louisville; and the cultivation of a two-year-old program that would spotlight the talents of racing's future stars.

The first race ever run at Keeneland was for two-year-old fillies at six furlongs, and the winner was Royal Raiment, a gray daughter of Royal Minstrel owned by John Hay Whitney, entrepreneur, philanthropist, and future ambassador to Great Britain.

Myrtlewood, owned by Keeneland director Brownell Combs, not only won on the same program, defeating one female and three male rivals while astoundingly giving from

Queen Elizabeth II visited Keeneland in 1984 and presented the trophy to Claiborne Farm's Seth Hancock for the race named in her honor.

fifteen to twenty-seven pounds, she captured the Ashland Stakes two days later. And on the meet's closing day, October 24, the bay daughter of Blue Larkspur defeated Whitney's Miss Merriment in a special match race while under a hand ride.

Fillies and mares have continued dazzling fans at Keeneland ever since. The significance of races for female runners is such that retired Keeneland chairman James E. "Ted" Bassett III — who served in various executive capacities for thirty-three years — named two distaff races in his list of Keeneland's top five landmark events: the inaugural runnings of the Spinster Stakes in 1956 and the Queen Elizabeth II Challenge Cup in 1984.

Proposed by Headley, the 1 1/8-mile Spinster was created to be a championship event for fillies and mares, becoming the first weight-for-age stakes for distaffers in America. Immediately, the Spinster lived up to Headley's ambitions, with Claiborne Farm's three-year-old homebred Doubledogdare winning over the accomplished five-year-old Queen

Hopeful and wrapping up the sophomore filly championship in the process.

Doubledogdare had both broken her maiden and won the Alcibiades Stakes at Keeneland the previous season, in which she reigned as the juvenile filly champion. And in the spring of 1956 she had won the Ashland Stakes, Keeneland's springboard to the Kentucky Oaks at Churchill Downs, in which she finished second. To commemorate Doubledogdare's outstanding record at Keeneland, track officials created a stakes race named in her honor in 1992, which was run at seven furlongs through 1994 but extended to 1 1/16 miles in 1998 after a hiatus of four years. Winners have included two-time American champion Silverbulletday and Canadian champion Dancethruthedawn.

Beyond Doubledogdare, the quality of the first Spinster field was further demonstrated by the fact that two unplaced runners, Delta and Levee, later distinguished themselves with Broodmare of the Year honors in 1968 and 1970, respectively.

Twenty-one additional American female champions have emerged from subsequent

The Ashland Stakes was named for the estate of Kentucky favorite son Henry Clay.

runnings of the Spinster, including the two-time winners Bornastar (1957, 1958), Susan's Girl (1973, 1975), and Bayakoa (1989, 1990). Many other champions, Breeders' Cup winners, and significant broodmares count the Spinster, which was made an elite grade I event when grading of stakes began in 1973, as one of their starts. Saudi Arabian Prince Khalid Abdullah's Juddmonte Farms, one of the world's most esteemed breeders, acknowledged the Spinster tradition when it began sponsoring the race in 2005.

With Keeneland's emphasis on races for fillies and mares, it is not surprising that six of the track's ten grade I races conducted in 2010 were restricted to female runners.

Another of those elite races, the Queen Elizabeth II Challenge Cup, has a far different history from the Spinster, having been created solely to honor Great Britain's monarch on her visit to Central Kentucky in 1984. Following nearly 18 months of preparation for the event and $3 million for an addition to the grandstand, Keeneland offered a purse of $106,625 for the initial running of the 1 1/16-mile race.

Go for Wand won the 1990 Ashland Stakes.

Bull Lea, who would become Calumet Farm's foundation sire, won an early running of the Blue Grass Stakes; below, an early Keeneland souvenir letter opener

Most importantly, however, Bassett recalls that the Queen's presence elevated the image of Keeneland around the world as a prestigious center of racing.

"I think that gave us sort of an international stamp of approval and raised the international perception that Keeneland was more than a sales company and just another racetrack," Bassett said.

"It was remarkable how the public responded and how people came from Louisville, Cincinnati, Nashville, and Chicago," he reflected. "There was quiet and respectable applause — no yelling of 'Hey, Queen!' — and little children waved British flags. And she was very impressed with the horses; she was quite taken."

Sintra, owned by the Cherry Valley Farm of Claiborne president Seth Hancock, won the inaugural running of the Challenge Cup by a nose from Solar Halo.

The very next year, Keeneland became the first racetrack in Kentucky to open a turf course, and the Queen Elizabeth II Challenge Cup was, appropriately considering its connection to England, moved to the grass, where it has stayed, although the distance was lengthened to 1 1/8 miles beginning in 1990. In 1991 the race

was designated an elite grade I event while the annual purse has risen fivefold to $500,000.

Female turf champions Ryafan (1997) and Perfect Sting (1999) both won the Queen Elizabeth II Challenge Cup in their championship seasons.

Keeneland's other grade I stakes races for distaffers are the Darley Alcibiades for juveniles, the Central Bank Ashland for three-year-olds, the Vinery Madison for older fillies and mares, and the First Lady for three-year-olds and up.

Named for Headley's foundation mare and ancestress of more than a dozen stakes winners, the Alcibiades was elevated to grade I status in 2007 following a star-studded history that began in 1952. Prominent winners in addition to Doubledogdare have spanned 1956 champion

Calumet Farm owner Warren Wright leads Whirlaway, winner of the 1941 Breeders' Futurity and second in the 1942 Blue Grass.

Mocassin won the 1965 Alcibiades for the Hancock family's Claiborne Farm.

juvenile filly Leallah, 1965 champion juvenile filly and co-Horse of the Year Moccasin, 1977 Canadian juvenile filly champion and Horse of the Year L'Alezane, 1992 champion juvenile filly Eliza, and 1997 and '98 champions Countess Diana and Silverbulletday.

Sheikh Mohammed bin Rashid al Maktoum's worldwide Darley breeding empire has backed the Alcibiades with sponsorship since 2003.

Dating back to the initial Keeneland meeting and Myrtlewood, the Ashland Stakes was named for the Lexington homestead and breeding establishment of statesman Henry Clay. This illustrious contest, which has been run at a variety of distances from six furlongs to the current 1 1/16 miles, has been a grade I race since 1986 and has spotlighted important fillies throughout its history. Lexington-based Central Bank became the title sponsor of the race in 2010.

Some of the Ashland's most prominent winners have been those fillies that went on to conquer the Kentucky Oaks: Valdina Myth (1941), Real Delight (1952), Sally Ship (1963), Blue Norther (1964), Sun and Snow (1975), Optimistic Gal (1976), Blush With Pride (1982), Princess Rooney (1983), and Silverbulletday (1999).

Go for Wand, who won the 1990 Ashland and was a two-time champion, earned induction in the Racing Hall of Fame alongside Princess Rooney and 1994 Ashland winner and champion Inside Information, while 1992 Ashland winner Prospectors Delite became 2003 Broodmare of the Year after her son, Mineshaft, earned Horse of the Year honors.

No recounting of outstanding Ashland winners would be complete, however, without Bewitch, Calumet Farm's phenomenal homebred dual champion who took the race in 1948, a year after she had defeated the mighty Citation in the Washington Park Futurity. Keeneland initiated the Bewitch Stakes to honor the daughter of Bull Lea in 1962 and it was run as a sprint through 1978. Although Bewitch's average winning distance was 6.77 furlongs, Keeneland lengthened the distance of the race named after her and since 1995 it has been run at 1 ½ miles on the turf.

CLASSIC BLUE GRASS TRADITIONS

While fillies have always been prized at Keeneland, male runners certainly have not been overshadowed. Primary among the track's major events annually is the Blue Grass Stakes, a key prep for the Kentucky Derby whose history dates back to 1911 at the Kentucky Association track.

Revived in 1937 during Keeneland's first spring meeting with a purse of $5,000, the Blue Grass was expected to be dominated by Colonel E. R. Bradley's duo of Billionaire and

Ridan left the field behind in the 1962 Blue Grass Stakes.

Impetuosity's win in 1971 headlined Keeneland's first day to top $1 million in total betting handle; below, note the Churchill Downs location for the 1943 Keeneland spring meet.

Brooklyn. However, Maxwell Howard's Fencing, apparently relishing sloppy conditions, upset Billionaire by three-quarters of a length in a yet another feat for trainer Earl Sande, the former champion jockey who had ridden Triple Crown winner Gallant Fox to glory. Sande would go on to rank as America's leading trainer in 1938.

In just its second renewal at Keeneland, the Blue Grass delivered a thrilling battle, with Calumet's Bull Lea prevailing by a neck over 1937 champion juvenile Menow in record-smashing time of 1:49 3/5 for the 1 1/8 miles. Both runners would achieve greater prominence in the breeding shed, with Bull Lea siring 1947 and '48 Blue Grass winners Faultless and Coaltown, respectively, as well as 1948 and 1952 Ashland winners Bewitch and Real Delight, while Menow got 1949 and 1953 Horses of the Year Capot and Tom Fool.

Shut Out, campaigned by the Greentree Stable of John Hay Whitney's mother, Mrs. Payne Whitney, and ridden by the incomparable Eddie Arcaro, became the first Blue Grass winner at Keeneland to triumph in the Kentucky Derby. Since his victory in 1942, nine other Blue Grass winners also have earned the roses in Louisville: Tomy Lee (1959), Chateaugay (1963), Northern Dancer (1964), Lucky Debonair (1965), Forward Pass (upon disqualification of Dancer's Image in 1968), Dust Commander (1970), Riva Ridge (1972), Spectacular Bid (1979), and Strike the Gold (1991).

Right, Holy Bull ran away from his rivals in the 1994 Blue Grass Stakes; below, Bill Shoemaker won many races at Keeneland.

But that list is just a beginning in terms of assessing the role of the Blue Grass in modern American classic history. Other Derby winners to have emerged from the race include Decidedly (1962), Proud Clarion (1967), Gato Del Sol (1982), Alysheba (1987), Unbridled (1990), Sea Hero (1993), Thunder Gulch (1995), and Street Sense (2007).

Preakness Stakes winners that competed in the Blue Grass include Bimelech in 1940, who triumphed at Keeneland while eighty-year-old owner E. R. Bradley watched from a black limousine parked in the clubhouse area at the head of the stretch. Both Bimelech and 1974 Blue Grass fourth-place finisher Little Current would sweep the Preakness and the Belmont Stakes.

Additional Preakness winners to have run in the Blue Grass were Faultless, Northern Dancer, Forward Pass, Spectacular Bid, Deputed Testamony, Alysheba, Summer Squall, Prairie Bayou, and Louis Quatorze. Other Belmont winners who competed in the Blue

Grass are Shut Out, Counterpoint, Sherluck, Chateaugay, Arts and Letters, Riva Ridge, Avatar, Thunder Gulch, Editor's Note, and Lemon Drop Kid.

Of all the Blue Grass graduates, however, none can top the charismatic Whirlaway, Calumet's flaming chestnut known as "Mr. Longtail" for his streaming banner of an appendage. Second in the Keeneland mud to Our Boots in the 1941 Blue Grass, Whirlaway proceeded to streak through the Triple Crown for trainer Ben Jones and jockey Arcaro.

Raised just a few furlongs down Versailles Road, Whirlaway enjoyed a bounty of success at Keeneland, winning the 1940 Breeders' Futurity during his juvenile championship season and the 1941 A. J. Joyner Handicap (one of a record twelve wins for Jones during the spring meet). The son of Blenheim II also competed at Keeneland in 1942, his second consecutive Horse of the Year campaign.

That season also marked the end of racing at Keeneland for three years as it was asked to close during World War II due to its designation as a "suburban" facility and an ongoing national rubber shortage. Keeneland's spring meet races were transferred to Churchill Downs from 1943-45.

Even with so many influential Triple Crown race winners, the Blue Grass can claim importance beyond those runners. For example, Round Table, who won the Blue Grass in 1957, went on to be North America's all-time leading money winner of his era and the Horse of the Year in 1958, while 1996 winner Skip Away went on to earn more than $9 million and the 1998 Horse of the Year title. Skip Away's victory also occurred in the first

Left, Charismatic used the 1999 Lexington Stakes as a springboard to a Derby victory; above, Keeneland's winningest jockey, Pat Day

The connections of 1962 Blue Grass Stakes winner Ridan, including trainer Leroy Jolley, left, accept the trophy.

year of race sponsorship by Toyota, which has continued to support the event and its current purse of $750,000.

Although the Blue Grass traditionally was run just nine days before the Kentucky Derby, it was moved beginning in 1989 to three weeks prior to the Run for the Roses to satisfy horsemen concerned that the two major races were too close together. Bassett said that shift on the calendar was one of the most significant decisions of his Keeneland administration, preserving the Blue Grass as a premier classic prep.

Bassett also rates several Blue Grass runnings as the most noteworthy races of Keeneland's modern era. Impetuosity's win in 1971 headlined Keeneland's first day to top $1 million in total betting handle. Skip Away set a Blue Grass record that was still standing after thirteen years with a time of 1:47 1/5 when he romped away from eventual classic winners Louis Quatorze and Editor's Note in a stellar rendition.

Pat Day, Keeneland's all-time winningest jockey by meet titles (twenty-two), victories (918), and stakes wins (ninety-five), captured his fourth Blue Grass trophy in 2000 aboard High Yield after a torrid head-and-head stretch battle with More Than Ready and his rider, John Velazquez. Day thus achieved a tie with Arcaro for second among all jockeys in the history of the race. Another legendary Hall of Famer, Bill Shoemaker, rode six Blue Grass winners — Tomy Lee (1959), Tompion (1960), Lucky Debonair (1965), Abe's Hope, who upset the previously unbeaten Graustark when that rival fractured a coffin bone in 1966, Arts and Letters (1969), and Linkage (1982).

One of the most memorable races in Keeneland's history occurred in the 1978 Blue Grass when Calumet's homebred Alydar won by a record 13 lengths after appearing to nod in deference to Admiral Gene and Lucille Markey of Calumet following the post parade. His win marked the sixth Blue Grass trophy collected by Calumet, which leads all owners by wins.

"The Markeys had never seen him before," Bassett said. "We had arranged for the Keeneland station wagon to be taken to Calumet. The Markeys were both aged and had difficulty getting through crowds, so we brought them to the clubhouse area and

Lucille Parker Markey and Gene Markey greeted Alydar before the 1978 Blue Grass Stakes.

Bugler Bucky Sallee
has been a
Keeneland fixture
for fifty years.

the fence next to the racetrack. (Jockey) Jorge Velasquez steered Alydar to the rail and the colt lowered his head."

"The horse bowed to her, unbelievably," Calumet secretary Margaret Glass said at the time. "She was thrilled."

Mrs. Markey raised a white-gloved hand and waved as Alydar galloped by her moments later, the easiest kind of winner as the 1-10 favorite. A son of Raise a Native and a great-grandson of Ashland winner Real Delight, Alydar would go on to finish second in each of Affirmed's Triple Crown race victories, earning a dubious distinction as the only horse ever to place in each of those storied events. Eventually, for a brief time, Affirmed and Alydar would stand at stud together at nearby Calumet, with Alydar gaining a measure of revenge while regarded as the superior sire.

Although the Blue Grass clearly is the jewel of Keeneland's spring meet, another major classic prep has been developed in the form of the Lexington Stakes. First run at the inaugural meeting in 1936 for juveniles and then made a handicap for three-year-olds and up from 1938-41, the Lexington was re-introduced to the stakes schedule in 1984, taking the place of the previously run Calumet Purse. International breeding giant Coolmore has sponsored the Lexington, a grade II event, since 1998.

Prominent winners of the 1 1/16-mile Lexington include 1999 Horse of the Year and Kentucky Derby and Preakness winner Charismatic, 1997 Belmont Stakes winner Touch Gold, and 1991 Preakness and Belmont winner Hansel.

YOUTH AND BEAUTY

Because Kentucky breeders have supported and cherished Keeneland from the beginning, it has been only logical that the track maintain a competitive program for juvenile runners, who carry breeders' most current aspirations and greatly impact the fortunes of young stallions.

Even today, many stables bring their best young stock to Keeneland in both the spring and the fall to test their mettle in juvenile races. In the 1970s, Millard Waldheim's Bwamazon Farm earned seven leading owner titles during the spring meet, primarily propelled by its precocious two-year-olds.

Horse of the Year
Favorite Trick
added the 1997
Breeders' Futurity
to his perfect record
as a juvenile.

Joining the Alcibiades as a crowning event for juveniles at Keeneland each autumn is the Breeders' Futurity, a grade I event contested at 1 1/16 miles and offering a purse of $500,000. Originally dating back to 1910 at the Kentucky Association track, the Breeders' Futurity was renewed at Keeneland in 1938, when, as a six-furlong dash, it was captured by Johnstown. Bearing the famed Belair Stud silks, Johnstown was bound for Kentucky Derby glory the following season.

In 1940 Whirlaway earned the Breeders' Futurity trophy and the race's prestige was cemented. Two-time champion and fellow Hall of Famer Devil Diver captured the race in 1941 for Greentree Stable and trainer John M. Gaver Sr., a future Hall of Famer who conditioned five classic winners and two Horse of the Year champions during his thirty-eight-year tenure with the Whitney family's Greentree operation.

Other notable winners of the Breeders' Futurity include Hasty Road, champion

Kip Deville won the Maker's Mark Mile in successive years; below, special limited edition bottles of Maker's Mark sell out in hours on Maker's Mark Mile Day.

juvenile of 1953; Round Table (1956); Swale, who would follow up his 1983 win with championship honors the next year and victories in the Kentucky Derby and Belmont; champion juvenile Tasso (1985); Forty Niner, who like Swale carried Claiborne's gold silks and who was champion juvenile in 1987; champion juvenile Boston Harbor (1996); and champion juvenile and Horse of the Year Favorite Trick (1997).

The Breeders' Futurity also has been a significant race in the Racing Hall of Fame career of D. Wayne Lukas, Keeneland's all-time leading trainer by wins (267 at the end of 2008), stakes wins (fifty), and meet titles (sixteen). Runners trained by Lukas, who was still saddling winners on his seventy-fifth birthday in September 2009, have won an unprecedented six editions of the Breeders' Futurity. Lukas also has taken a trophy home from many of Keeneland's other headline events, including four from the Lexington Stakes, three from the Ashland, and two from the Blue Grass. Dixiana Farm became the title sponsor of the grade I race in 2009.

RACING ON THE TURF

While two-year-old racing is a hallowed tradition, turf racing is relatively new at Keeneland, following the installation of the grass course — the first in Kentucky — in 1985. However, racing over turf has grown to be a major focus at Keeneland, with the grade I Shadwell Turf Mile, worth $600,000, an annual feature of the fall meet that, like the Queen Elizabeth II Challenge Cup, lures international runners. Sponsored by Sheikh Hamdan bin Rashid al Maktoum's hallmark breeding farm, the Turf Mile was initiated in 1986 and has been won by turf champions Steinlen (1989) and Itsallgreektome (1991).

Maker's Mark, the world-famous bourbon distiller based in Loretto, Kentucky, also has partnered with Keeneland in the development of a

top-level turf event. The Maker's Mark Mile Stakes (formerly the Fort Harrod Stakes), run annually during the spring meeting since 1989 and carrying a purse of $300,000 in 2010, has been a launching pad for no less than four winners of the international championship-caliber Breeders' Cup Mile: Opening Verse (1991), Artie Schiller (2005), Miesque's Approval (2006), and Kip Deville (2007). In leaving his own mark on the Maker's Mark, Kip Deville returned to win the race again in 2008, becoming the only two-time winner to date. With this kind of a record, the Maker's Mark Mile gained grade I status in 2008.

While extending its race sponsorship into a growing social gathering attracting bourbon connoisseurs from around the country, Maker's Mark has worked creatively with Keeneland for the betterment of the local community raising more than $5 million to date for causes ranging from cancer research and Thoroughbred retirement to educational and cultural outreach to children across Kentucky. This has been accomplished through the sale of a special limited edition bottle released across Kentucky on Keeneland's opening day each spring. Those bottles sell out within hours and well over a thousand fans return the following Friday, on Maker's Mark Mile Day, in hopes of having those bottles signed.

Kelly's Landing used a victory in the 2006 Phoenix Stakes as a springboard to international success.

The high-tech tote board helps fans pinpoint horses' positions in every phase of a race.

Two stakes for juveniles on the turf — the Bourbon for colts and the JP Morgan Chase Jessamine for fillies, each at 1 1/16 miles — are run during the fall. Other fall turf races are the 1 1/16 mile Pin Oak Valley View for three-year-old fillies followed by the 1 1/2 mile Rood & Riddle Dowager for three-year-old and up fillies and mares.

In the spring, two stakes for four-year-olds and up run on the turf are the Grey Goose Bewitch (for fillies and mares) and the Fifth Third Elkhorn — both at 1 1/2 miles. The overall progression of turf racing at Keeneland is such that during 2009 a total of nineteen stakes, representing more than half of the track's thirty-six listed and graded events, were conducted on grass. Two stakes for juveniles on the turf — the Bourbon for colts and the JP Morgan Chase Jessamine for fillies, each at 1 1/16 miles — are run during the fall.

FALL RACING

Another highlight of Keeneland's autumn meeting is the Phoenix Stakes, a six-furlong sprint for three-year-olds and up that holds the grand distinction of being the oldest stakes race in the United States. First run in 1831 at the Kentucky Association track and named after a landmark hotel that opened in Lexington in the 1820s, the stakes was first run at Keeneland in the spring of 1937. Conducted at Churchill Downs during the

World War II years, the Phoenix initially served as a spring fixture and one of several preparatory races for the classic season until it was shifted on the calendar in 1989.

Prominent winners of the Phoenix, a grade III event with a 2009 purse of $250,000, include Devil Diver (1942), Coaltown (1948), Hill Gail, who rocketed from his track-record equaling victory in 1:10 2/5 in 1952 to win that year's Kentucky Derby, Moccasin (1967), champion Gallant Bob (1976), champion filly Xtra Heat (2002), American record-equaling miler Najran (2003), and Kelly's Landing (2006), who went on to reign as champion sprinter in the United Arab Emirates after winning the $2-million Dubai Golden Shaheen in 2007.

Rounding out the fall meet are a number of graded races including the seven-furlong Raven Run, first run in 1999. Lexus became the title sponsor in 2005 for this grade II race named after a 374-acre nature sanctuary outside of Lexington. The Perryville Stakes, a seven-furlong, 184-foot race for 3 year olds named for the 1862 Civil War Battle of Perryville fought thirty miles southwest of Lexington, has been underwritten by Budweiser Select since 2005.

There have been an infinite number of additional milestone occasions as racing at Keeneland has evolved. Among the events Bassett cited as most significant were the installation of Polytrack in 2006 to safeguard the welfare of horses and jockeys; the implementation of a track public address system and the hiring of announcer Kurt Becker in 1997; and the switch from specialized

Keeneland is designated a National Historic Landmark while at the same time boasting many state-of-the-art features; the main track shortly before the Polytrack cushion (surface) was laid down

betting windows to all cash and sell windows in 1979, again leading the way with that innovation in Kentucky.

The many enhancements of Keeneland's facilities included an extension of the grandstand in 1953 and the addition of nearly 4,000 seats. At that time, the finish line was moved 184 feet closer to the track's first turn, resulting in a lengthening of the stretch run from 990 to 1,174 feet. This change allowed the Beard Course — so called in honor of Major Louis A. Beard, who had led the volunteer committee that selected the site for Keeneland — to be established at seven furlongs and 184 feet. The Headley Course, named after the track's first president, was increased from less than a half-mile to four furlongs and 152 feet (before a later change made it 4½ furlongs).

In recognition of its incomparable traditions, Keeneland was saluted with the designation of national historic landmark in 1986.

While so much has changed over the years — including growth to previously unimaginable levels such as the expansion of the grounds to 1,024 acres; the admission of a record 244,145 fans to the seventeen-day 2006 fall meet that featured the unveiling of Polytrack, wider turns, a longer stretch run, and a new tote board; the record total of $158,368,308 wagered during the 2007 spring meet; and average daily purses that are among the highest in North America — Keeneland's racing program nonetheless has remained true to the founders' wishes. Keeneland has kept its meets brief so they will be treasured and amply supported by fans, purse revenues, and owners. While the spring meet offers essential preparation for the classics, the fall meet has risen to be a valuable precursor to the Breeders' Cup championship races that were inaugurated in 1984.

As the track's racing has prospered even while the march of development has changed the face of Lexington and America as a whole, Keeneland's landscape seems more and more like a magical shrine to the Thoroughbred and those who have fostered the breed. Famed for stately trees, which erupt in a profusion of color during both spring and fall racing meets, and for the champions that continue to grace its barns and paths, Keeneland is indeed like no other racetrack.

"Keeneland should be the national park of racing," reflected the late Howard Battle, who served as racing secretary from 1973 until shortly before his death in 2002. "The beauty of spring with the clean, clear air and the blooms of the pears, crab apples and dogwoods are excelled only in October by the yellows, golds, ambers, oranges and reds of the same flora. Besides the aesthetic atmosphere and the multitudinous contradictions to most racing establishments — (including) being near the horses in their natural setting — (Keeneland) is still the best road to the Kentucky Derby and Oaks and now the Breeders' Cup."

THE TURF CLUB
AT KEENELAND Sue Wylie

I t is an hour before post time at Keeneland and cars full of happy race-goers are streaming into the track. Most of them turn toward the grandstand and the general parking areas. But some cars with special decals on their windshields are waved on into a special lane that leads to the members-only Keeneland Clubhouse where parking valets stand at attention to whisk them away. Inside the handsome stone building there is a well-dressed crowd and a well-mannered hub-bub of "hellos" and "how are you's." Hands are shaken, cheeks are kissed as club members greet each other and mingle in the charming, spacious reception room before heading up the soft-carpeted stairs to their members-only boxes or luncheon tables, which wait, reserved and ready, draped in immaculate starched linen. The gleam of the table silver is matched by the communal glow of geniality that hovers around this crowd of "members only" and their guests for the day.

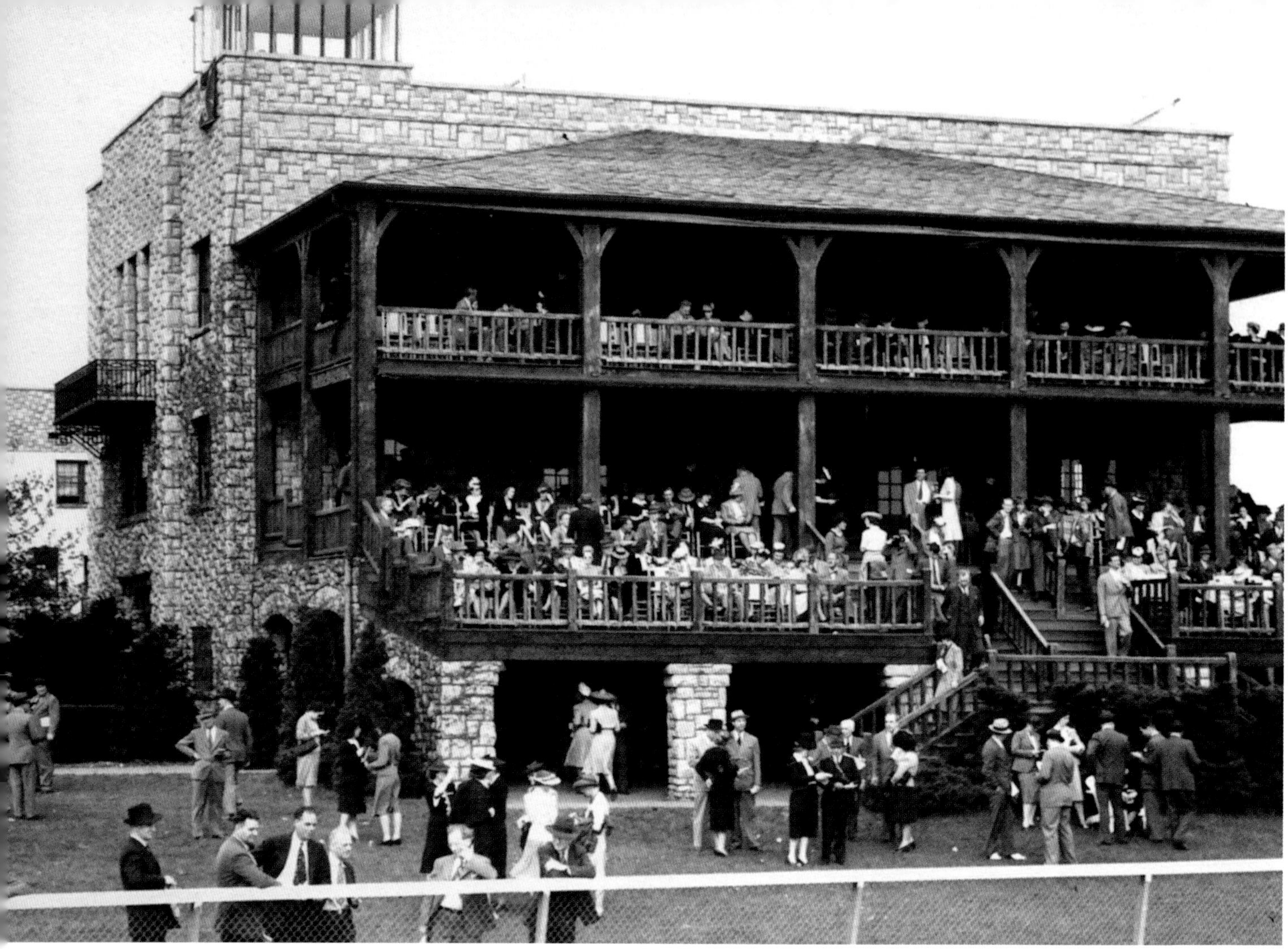

From the start Keeneland sought "wholesome people" to be club members; right, Beard talks with jockey Eddie Arcaro, one of the many famous riders who have competed at the track.

If the men who founded Keeneland Race Course and created this members-only club three-quarters of a century ago could stand in the clubhouse today, they would surely wear wide smiles of satisfaction. Spearheaded by Major Louie A. Beard, this was part of their long-ago dream: a permanent, private club that would carry on the camaraderie and hospitality of early racing traditions. Now, seventy-five years later, the club is internationally renowned in racing circles for its conviviality and graciousness. Even one visit will leave guests with life-long wistful memories of their wonderful day at Keeneland.

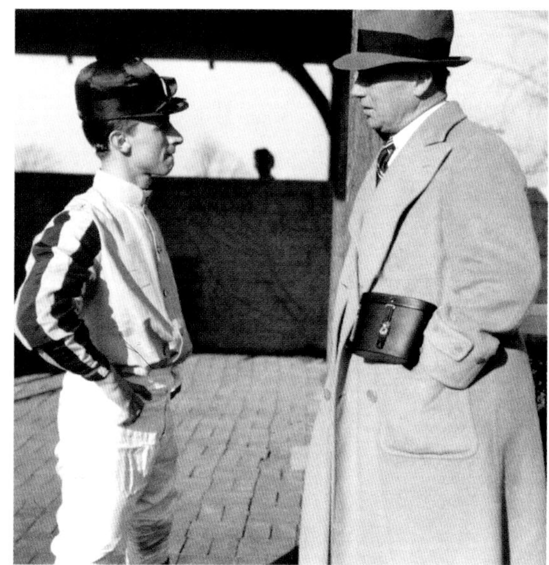

From the beginning, these founding fathers assured the public that while the Keeneland Club would always be private, it would never be elitist. They made that clear in one of their first announcements printed in *The Blood-Horse* in May 1936. It stated, "The prime idea is that the Keeneland Club shall be composed of wholesome people regardless of their birth or social or business standing." Although the membership roster was then, and still is today, heavily sprinkled with the names of prominent horse owners and breeders, being part of the equine industry is not the only requisite for membership, according to James E. "Ted" Bassett III, the former longtime president of Keeneland and now retired chairman.

Memberships in the Keeneland Club are highly prized.

"We do try to give preference to people who buy, sell, or race with us and there is some preference of family members, but mostly we simply look for people who will appreciate and honor its traditions."

So, why, then, doesn't every racing fan join the Keeneland Club and enjoy its delicious privileges, pleasures, and perks? The answer is one word: space. There's just not enough of it. The club began with only ninety members. There are now more than 1,000, and Nick Nicholson, who wears dual crowns as Keeneland president and CEO, says they all must be accommodated in style and comfort, with no overcrowding.

"It's very frustrating for a member *not* to be able to reserve a table," he said. "But even

The rail of the clubhouse lawn provides a perfect vantage point for watching the races.

now we have to limit requests for reservations. During the meets, we have eight people in our ticket office who spend 100 percent of their time just juggling Club requests. Every day, when I walk through the club dining rooms, I hear stories of people who, literally, plan their year around April and October and the Keeneland Club."

In the clubhouse office, files hold at least 1,000 applications for membership. Some have been on the waiting list for years. More than 100 new applications are received each year and the discouraging news is that only a few of those are approved. The disappointed others go back on the list to wait another year, at the very least.

The process does take patience … lots of it. Each applicant must be sponsored, in writing, by two club members and approved by the membership committee which meets just once a year and whose names are never given out. Membership, or being a guest of a member, is the only way to gain admission to the clubhouse. No one, prince or president, can pay his or her way in, as allowed by many other track clubs.

Nicholson shook his head and laughed. "The strange thing is that the tougher it is to get in, the more people want in. There is a definite mystique to the Keeneland Club and they want to be part of it. There's an aura that attracts them like a magnet."

"Membership drive" and "Keeneland Club" would seem the ultimate oxymoron but,

CELEBRATING 75 YEARS OF TRADITION

Then as now, race-goers in general and club members in particular take pride in their racing attire.

yes, there was such a thing back in the spring of 1936 as construction crews were readying Keeneland Race Course for its debut race meet in October. Everything was on schedule and the visionaries of the new track decided it was time to tackle another dream. They had the plan, and the place. All they needed were the people. So in the last week of April, handsomely engraved invitations began showing up in mailboxes not only in Kentucky but from coast to coast, with special attention paid to the Cincinnati area and the members of the Carmargo Polo Club. Bearing the impressive gold seal of the Keeneland Association and accompanied by a letter from the president, Hal Price Headley, here was an invitation to become a founding member of a landmark new club. The fee for a life membership for "one gentleman and one woman" would be $500. "No further dues or assessments" … ever!

Ninety people accepted that invitation, unaware that it would turn out to be one of the biggest bargains of their lives. As of 2010, Keeneland Club dues were set at $900 annually for married couples and $600 for single members *except*, that is, for the fortunate heirs to those original ninety memberships, of which seventy are still in use. Only those members are entitled to the prestigious, dime-sized white "life member pins," which they wear

with the deep pride of being part of racing history. Ironically, some of the original members had to be persuaded to join. Today, a Keeneland Club Life membership is a cherished family treasure, often passed down from one generation to another along with great-grandmother's crystal punch bowl.

While only a few may wear "life member pins," all members are entitled to wear handsome, colorful medallion pins as their admission badges to the private clubrooms. Since 1968, the pins have been designed each year to honor an owner or farm that has

helped build Keeneland's impeccable worldwide reputation. The colors of the pins are inspired by the honoree's racing silks. Members are mailed their new pins each spring along with a small card describing the silks and the owner's racing or sales contributions to Keeneland. Men receive round club buttons; the ladies version is the same button attached to a small enameled bar. The pins are so attractive they often end up, after racing season, made into cuff links or charm bracelets to be worn year round.

The glamour and allure that set the Keeneland Club apart from other tracks begins at its front door, and Ted Bassett knows why. In his decades as a top Keeneland executive, he has watched the surprised and delighted faces of thousands of guests as they stepped into the main reception room.

"The first impression is that you've entered a lovely, private family living room in a beautiful home in a rural atmosphere," he said. "There are fresh-cut flowers, big easy chairs, and a huge handsome stone fireplace. There is a touch of elegance and sophistication. It looks and feels like a home. There is nothing commercial about it. From day one, the emphasis of the club has always been on quality and not quantity. For example, we could have put much more furniture in the room to seat more people, but then, we would have sacrificed the home-like atmosphere.

Ever since Beard chose the classic oak and leather furniture back in 1936, the clubhouse always has been about grace, never gimmicks. It's very tempting to tinker or tamper with things in the name of "keeping up to date" but, thankfully, that has not been the fate of the clubhouse. Instead, photographs show its decor today is very much like the original. In the mid-1950s, famed interior designer Billy Baldwin was brought in to work his magic. Although he was known as the "decorating darling of the New York smart set," Baldwin wisely understood the unpretentious, comfortable ambiance of the Keeneland Club.

"It's so very personal. I felt like I was doing a big country Southern home with absolutely no commercial feeling," he said later.

It was Baldwin who brought in the inviting, deep-cushioned couches and chairs, covered them with simple printed cottons, and brightened the room with patterned

Alma Haggin, wife of Keeneland president Louis Lee Haggin II, had exacting standards for how the racetrack should look; opposite, the towering centerpiece in the clubhouse lobby and fresh flowers elsewhere in the club are Keeneland traditions.

CELEBRATING 75 YEARS OF TRADITION

draperies and rugs. Over the years he returned time and again to "freshen' up" the entire clubhouse from dining rooms to powder rooms. After his retirement, Baldwin's protégé and later business partner, Arthur Smith, handled Keeneland's interior design needs until his untimely death in 1997. The baton was then passed to nationally known designer William Hodgins of Boston. Hodgins, too, approached the Keeneland Club as though it were a private home. His low-key, tailored "re-workings," as he called them, of Baldwin's interiors were very discreet, and kept the continuity of the beloved Keeneland style. One must realize Baldwin and Hodgins were both super-successful designers, sought by high-profile clients around the world who would give them free rein. Their high-paid decorating decisions were rarely questioned *until* they came to Lexington and met up with Alma Haggin, whose approval of any changes at Keeneland was all-important.

Not enough can be said about the enormous influence this dignified unofficial mistress of Keeneland had on everything from the lush landscaping to the crispness of the dining room table linens. The Keeneland look is mainly the result of her exquisite eye for detail.

Clubhouse fans still flock to the rail to watch the action.

From childhood until her death in 2005, Keeneland was a major part of Haggin's daily life. Her father, Hal Price Headley, co-founded the track. Her husband, Thoroughbred owner and breeder Louis Lee Haggin II, was Keeneland's second president, and their son, Louis Lee Haggin III, is a Keeneland trustee and director. In the track's early hard-scratch years, there was not even a penny of money for frills such as designers or decorators so Alma Haggin herself volunteered to make sure everything would be perfect everyday. Then, for more than sixty years, she confidently poured her own impeccable taste and design talents into making Keeneland one of the world's most beautiful racetracks. She insisted on bringing in only the finest, nationally recognized experts from architects to decorators, and then made sure, in the most gracious of ways, that *their* ideas matched *her* idea of how Keeneland should always look: classic, simple, under-stated with never a hint of ostentation. Decorators Baldwin and later Hodgins won her stamp of full approval.

"More than anyone else, Alma Haggin deserves the credit for creating the Keeneland standards of dignity, charm, and beauty," Bassett said. "What's more, she did it all as a labor of love. She never held an official title and was never compensated in any way."

It was Haggin's personal passion for gardening that created the most famous tradition of the clubhouse — the legendary flower arrangements in the lobby that make visitors stop dead in their tracks to ooh-and-ah and whip out their cameras. She decreed that the clubhouse rooms must always be bright with masses of blossoms on racing days and chose Lexington florist John Howard of Howard-Doyle (originally Howard & Heafey) to help her design and create oversized floral masterpieces, some using as many as 500 blooms. Together, they also planted the enchanting bright little garden on the clubhouse balcony. It's not easy to impress royalty, but the flowers are so spectacular they won the open admiration of Queen Elizabeth herself during her 1986 visit to Keeneland.

"We are special because we are different and it's Mrs. Haggin's elegant exquisite touches that make the difference," Bassett said. "For example, it was her idea to provide club members with little white silk French parasols to protect them from the sun or rain as they watch the races from their boxes. No other racetrack does that. It's a unique Keeneland tradition. Ours alone." (Note: The Keeneland Club also has another famously unique feature. It is world-known for having the absolutely worst view of the finish

Ladies Club pin
from 1977

line of *any* racetrack *anywhere*! Members simply laugh, shrug, and shake their heads indulgently over this. After all, no one is perfect … not even their beloved Keeneland.)

While none of the original founders of the Keeneland Club are left to celebrate its seventy-fifth anniversary, there is one man who was there at its inaugural day and is still a very active part of the clubhouse operation. Larry Wolken was just six years old on October 15, 1936, when he accompanied his father to the Keeneland opening.

"My dad owned Turf Catering and he took me to work with him that day," Wolken said. "I remember how exciting it was. It still is. I grew up to take over the business, and now the third generation, my sons Mike and Brad, are running it." He said with a proud smile. "Turf Catering is the only food concessionaire Keeneland has ever used, so we must be doing something right."

Wolken was responsible for coming up with the most popular items on the clubhouse menu: burgoo and bread pudding. "Those are our signature items. Those are the ones the members can't get enough of. I got the burgoo recipe from the old Idle Hour Farm, which is long gone, and for the bread pudding I traveled to New Orleans and personally met Chef Paul Prudhomme back in the seventies. I'm bragging, but Keeneland's pudding is better than his," Wolken said with a wink. "I make sure the bourbon sauce really tastes like bourbon."

If there was a "suggestions" box in the clubhouse, chances are it would stay empty. The members like things just the way they are

"We often conducted customer surveys," Bassett said. "We asked members what changes and improvements they would like to see. The answer was, 'Don't change *anything*!' "

But, of course, life and times do move on and there have been some changes in

Parasols shade racegoers from the rising sun in the outdoor boxes of the grandstand.

clubhouse rules and traditions, most recently in 1997 with the track-wide introduction of an announcer calling races over a public address system. Though some club members grumbled, the complaints quickly subsided.

Perhaps a more revolutionary change occurred in the 1970s, when the national fashion world decided that pants were now the new and so-chic replacement for women's skirts. The trend tore across the nation like wildfire. Suddenly, stylish women were wearing pants to the office, weddings, funerals, parties, banquets, and balls. But *not* to the Keeneland Clubhouse. Any woman member or guest who dared to show up in trousers was turned away with a polite, but stern reminder of the club's strict dress code. Women *must* be "suitably attired" and that meant in a skirt. That was the ironclad rule, until 1975. Bassett remembers its long-overdue demise:

"One day, Anita Madden, the glamorous matron of Hamburg Place horse farm, arrived at the clubhouse with a big entourage of important

The lawn and patio of the clubhouse beckon racegoers on sunny days.

out-of-town guests. She was wearing a beautiful, haute couture pants suits but she was stopped at the door and told she couldn't come in. So, she simply stepped into the ladies room, took off the pants, and re-appeared wearing only her jacket as a knee-length dress. She passed muster, too. That incident made us begin to realize how ridiculous the rule was and it was dropped soon after that."

But a strict dress code is still in effect in the clubhouse with no exceptions. Men *must* wear coats and ties. No turtlenecks, no open collars allowed, no denim garments of any kind for men *or* women, and no sneakers or tennis shoes ("Unless you have a broken foot," Bassett said).

Stationed right inside the clubhouse door, on every racing day, Lucy Bergen is a

The children of club members and their guests get an early education in Keeneland racing.

fetching sight with her white hair, bright blue eyes, and rosy cheeks. Decked out in her green Keeneland blazer and crisp white shirt, she smilingly greets arriving crowds.

"Welcome to Keeneland! Have a great day," she sings out. But Bergen is giving all who enter more than just a cheery greeting. She is also giving them the once-over … a discreet but eagle-eyed neck-to-toe inspection. Lucy, you see, is Keeneland's official "dress-coder" and she's tough.

"It's my job to see that everyone is properly dressed," she said proudly. "You'd be surprised how many men have to be told to, please, take your necktie out of your pocket and put it on. Nowadays we do allow strapless dresses in the club house but sometimes a lady will have on something that shows too much skin and then I have to stop her."

In such emergencies, Bergen is like the U.S. Coast Guard: always prepared. She has a private changing closest stocked with appropriate clothing for men and women.

There was a time when Keeneland was criticized, even ridiculed, for clinging to its dress code. "Stuffy," "old-fashioned," many people sniffed, but today, surprisingly, the younger racing fans are very strong supporters of the tradition. Even though their generation grew up in a world of "casual Fridays" and no neckties, they happily "dress up" and turn out in droves to see and be seen in the fashionable clubhouse crowds.

Lunch in the clubhouse can offer an intriguing smorgasbord of company. At one table might be the governor of Kentucky and a United States senator. At the next table might be a two-year old toddler and his teddy bear, because children as young as babes in arms are not only allowed in the clubhouse, their families are encouraged to bring them.

"From its beginning, the club has always strived for a very wholesome family atmosphere," Bassett explained. "Children have always been welcome. We hope that they'll be so fascinated by the horses that they grow up to be part of the industry themselves or, at least, lifelong racing fans," He laughed. "Besides, the clubhouse is a great place for them to watch a lot of grown-up people, all properly dressed and using proper etiquette at the table. It's a good lesson in manners.

After a decade as Keeneland president, Nicholson is sure the reason for the club's unique conviviality is "balance."

"We work very hard to make the membership a balanced mix. The club is partly horse people, of course, but there are also a lot of business leaders and professionals. Many of the club's original members were from Cincinnati and Louisville so we always try to remember people from those areas and, yes, we definitely keep balance in mind whenever we're able to take in a few new members."

Bassett summed it up like this: "Being part of the Keeneland Club is much more than just being social. It helps families plant their roots deeper in the community but more than that, it gives many people who would otherwise have no connection to the Thoroughbred world, a personal link to Kentucky's signature industry."

Perhaps the crowning compliment to the club came from Alice Headley Chandler, owner of Mill Ridge Farm and one of the Thoroughbred industry's most influential figures. She was just a little girl when her father, Hal Price Headley, co-founded the Keeneland racetrack and the club

"I've always watched it very carefully all the years since then," she said. "And I think Daddy would be absolutely thrilled with the club today. I feel we have grown and risen with great taste."

So, at the venerable age of seventy-five, the Keeneland Club is still the belle of the racing world ball ... that gorgeous girl everyone wants to dance with.

SUCCESS IN THE AUCTION RING

DEIRDRE B. BILES

Keeneland is the mightiest oak of equine commerce, but it all began with only a tiny acorn of an idea from Keeneland's creators. When they founded the track in the mid-1930s, they proposed conducting horse sales as part of the original prospectus. But it's doubtful Hal Price Headley, Major Louie A. Beard, and Keeneland's other early leaders ever imagined even in their wildest dreams how many billons of dollars would be generated by the company's auctions and how much of a worldwide impact its sales would have. The Keeneland of today is a huge global marketplace, selling more Thoroughbreds for more money than any other auction firm in the world.

Right, catalogs for the Keeneland September yearling sale, the largest auction of its kind; below, buyers examine horses in the November breeding stock sale.

During the most recent Thoroughbred auction boom, business at Keeneland peaked in 2007, when 9,124 horses were sold for $815,401,000 during its January horses of all ages, April juvenile, September yearling, and November breeding stock auctions. In 2008, buyers from nearly fifty states and forty-seven countries purchased Thoroughbreds at Keeneland, which offers everything from blue-blooded equines with the exclusivity of Tiffany gems to blue-collar horses that work hard for their money in claiming races.

Middle Eastern rulers shop at Keeneland, and so do captains of industry, oil tycoons, cowboys, automobile dealers, accountants, attorneys, doctors, and owners of small mom-and-pop farms, who rub elbows as they search the barns for good-looking prospects with genes that program them to run fast.

Keeneland's sale graduates, through 2010, included seventeen Kentucky Derby winners, eighteen Preakness winners, and sixteen Belmont Stakes winners.

Horses sold at Keeneland have won Breeders' Cup World Championship races, Epsom Irish and French Derbies, and the Dubai World Cup while earning numerous championships here and abroad.

Two-time Horses of the Year Curlin and John Henry were Keeneland graduates. The former brought $57,000 and the latter was offered twice as a young horse, bringing $1,100 in 1976 and $2,200 in 1977.

At the other end of the auction spectrum price-wise, are Seattle Dancer and Ashado. Seattle Dancer holds the world Thoroughbred auction record for a yearling after selling at Keeneland for $13.1 million in 1985. Until 2006, the handsome son of Nijinksky II, out of Triple Crown winner Seattle Slew's dam My Charmer, was the most expensive Thoroughbred ever sold anywhere. Ashado, who brought $9 million at Keeneland in 2005, is the planet's highest-priced broodmare prospect to date.

Such amazing figures for prime horseflesh, however, were inconceivable when the first sale of Thoroughbreds was conducted at Keeneland on April 25, 1938, under the

Above, champion Ashado brought a record $9 million; below, John Henry, who sold twice at Keeneland, once for $1,100, was one of racing's greatest bargains.

management of the famous auctioneer E.J. Tranter and his Lexington representative, Thomas Cromwell. Thirty-four horses were sold, grossing $24,885 and averaging $802.74. E.F. Woodward, who owned Valdina Farm near Valdina, Texas, paid the top price of $3,500 for a nine-year-old brown mare named Marmitina, and the suckling Cohort chestnut colt at her side. Horace N. Davis, agent, was their consignor.

Early yearling sales at Keeneland were conducted under a tent.

KEENELAND AUCTIONEERS

George Swinebroad, the big-voiced dean of Thoroughbred auctioneers, joined the Breeders' Sales Company when it was founded in 1944 and became Keeneland's first director of auctions. An imposing figure on the podium, Swinebroad was known for his quick tempo auctioneering style and clever prodding of buyers. He sold more than one billion dollars in bloodstock during his career, including nine yearlings that went on to win the Kentucky Derby, and was credited with establishing the bid-spotting system.

From left, Doc Bond, Humphrey Finney, and George Swinebroad preside at the auctioneer's stand in 1950. Below, the 1959 fall breeders sale

After Swinebroad's death in 1975, his protégé **Tom Caldwell**, who began selling Thoroughbreds at Keeneland in 1956, became the next director of auctions. The Caldwell name has been synonymous with the Keeneland sales, as Tom's two sons, Scott and Chris, flanked him on the podium for nearly three decades. The elder Caldwell hammered down more than eleven billion in sales during his career — including the $13.1 million sale of the yearling later named Seattle Dancer — and kept a perfect attendance record at Keeneland. Upon his death in 2001, fellow auctioneer **Ryan Mahan** was named senior auctioneer, a position he holds ten years later, while Scott and Chris continue on the podium to this day.

KEENELAND SALES DIRECTORS

The Breeders' Sales Company merged with the Keeneland Association and Keeneland Race Course in 1962 to form a single corporate enterprise. Keeneland Association became the operating company, with its auction division headed by **William S. Evans**. Evans remained at the helm of the sales until his retirement in 1980. The next director would not come aboard until 1982, when **W.B. Rogers Beasley** took over the position. Beasley remained the director of sales until 2001, when he moved on to become the director of racing. The assistant director of sales at the time, **Geoffrey Russell**, was promoted to his current role as director.

Approximately two hundred people attended the auction.

World War II, which changed the world in so many ways, also caused a major shift in the Thoroughbred marketplace, leading to the start of annual yearling sales at Keeneland. Prior to the major conflict, many Kentucky breeders shipped their yearlings to New York each summer and sold them through Fasig-Tipton. However, because of a wartime restriction on rail transportation, Bluegrass breeders were forced to keep their young horses at home. In 1943 Fasig-Tipton conducted an auction under a circus tent in the Keeneland paddock.

The sale, which was front-page news in the *Lexington Herald*, ran for three days, August 9-11. There were two sessions in the afternoon and evening daily. The 312 yearlings that sold averaged $2,980. According to *The Blood-Horse*, the Keeneland average, with resales included, was "almost exactly three times as high as the comparable figure at Saratoga in New York in 1942. With resales excluded, the average was 198 percent greater than Saratoga's 1942 average."

Keeneland's top-priced yearling brought $66,000, which was the highest price for a Thoroughbred of that age in this country since one had sold for $75,000 in 1928. But it was another yearling, a bay colt by Sir Gallahad III, that would develop into the auction's best racehorse. He sold for $10,000 to Fred W. Hooper, who was buying his first Thoroughbred and liked the way the colt looked and walked. Named Hoop Jr.,

the yearling went on to win the 1945 Kentucky Derby, and his new owner, who lived to the age of 102, became one of this country's most successful breeders and owners.

Not long after Keeneland's first yearling auction, Kentucky breeders, led by Claiborne Farm's Arthur B. Hancock, met in Lexington and decided to continue to sell their young horses locally on a permanent basis and build a sale pavilion on Keeneland's property. When Fasig-Tipton officials decided not to conduct the 1944 edition of the auction, Hancock and Headley spearheaded the creation of a co-op organization known as the Breeders' Sales Company.

Breeders' Sales purchased a horse sales arena that formerly had been owned by Fasig-Tipton from L.R. Cooke and Ben P. Eubank of Lexington and announced it would be dismantled and taken to Keeneland, according to a story that appeared in *The Thoroughbred Record* in April 1944.

Top and middle, the sales pavilion in the 1940s; above, an expanded sales pavilion, 1952.

The 1944 edition of the Keeneland summer yearling sale generated an average of $5,231, which was a North American record. It also sold two yearlings that became champion juveniles in 1945 the colt Star Pilot and the filly Beaugay. Their accomplishments helped boost Keeneland's reputation as a source of quality runners, and the auction firm continued to build on that distinction in the 1950s and 1960s.

The 1952 yearling auction produced all three winners of the 1954 Triple Crown: Determine (Kentucky Derby), Hasty Road (Preakness), and High Gun (Belmont Stakes). In 1961 Keeneland sold its first six-figure yearling, Swapson, who brought $130,000, which then was a world record. Humphrey Finney purchased Swapson for John Olin, but illness kept the colt with the lofty price from achieving greatness. He won six of his twenty-two career races and earned only $21,245.

In addition to selling yearlings, Keeneland expanded its offerings by starting a fall

CELEBRATING 75 YEARS OF TRADITION

Greek shipping magnate Stavros Niarchos, right, discusses a purchase with advisor Sir Philip Payne-Gallwey during the 1981 July selected yearling sale. Niarchos paid $9,575,000 for twenty-two yearlings during the two-day sale.

mixed sale in 1944 and a January mixed auction in the mid-1950s. Keeneland also sold yearlings in the fall, first as a part of the mixed sale and later in a separate auction that was moved to the month of September in 1960.

The Breeders' Sales Company ceased to exist 1962 when it was merged with the Keeneland Association and Keeneland Race Course into a single corporate enterprise. Under the new structure, Keeneland Association became the operating company and it had three divisions: an

auction division headed by William S. Evans, general manager, and George Swinebroad, director of sales; a racing division headed by general manager W.T. Bishop; and a publicity and public relations division overseen by J.B. Faulconer.

Late in the decade, the Keeneland Association spent $700,000 to build a new twelve-sided sale pavilion with 650 theater-style seats for consignors and buyers, bench-type seats for 150 spectators, and an exterior of limestone and glass.

A weak U.S. dollar in the 1970s helped attract an influx into Keeneland of foreign buyers, including Kazuo Nakamura of Japan and Greek shipping magnate Stavros Niarchos. With new customers to impress, consignors to the summer yearling auction stepped up their marketing efforts. In 1976, Kent Hollingsworth of *The Blood-Horse* wrote: "For many Julys at Keeneland, about the only device lending distinction to a consignment, other than the color in which the stall-door pedigree signs were painted, and the only amenities provided lookers, were shaded benches and water coolers located within walking rings. Then one year, a consignor offered iced Cokes, which caused some lookers to tarry longer and see more than one yearling in a consignment they had intended to inspect. The next year, a seller presented a champagne consignment. Tack room cocktails soon became commonplace at yearling showings."

According to Hollingworth, consignors in 1976 enticed buyers with a movie in a tack room, ice cream, sherbet, brown bags containing six small bottles of sauce, the opportunity to view an "extraordinary collection of gold cups," and a gold cup "on which a winning pari-mutuel ticket on Secretariat's Belmont Stakes was affixed."

Triple Crown winner Secretariat's first crop of yearlings was being offered at public auction, and Texas oil magnate and silver mogul Nelson Bunker Hunt had what nearly everyone considered to be the best of the bunch in his Bluegrass Farm sale barn. Secretariat's trainer, Lucien Laurin, declared the half-brother to champion Dahlia looked like his magnificent chestnut sire, and, according to *The Blood-Horse*, at least four different syndicates were put together to buy the colt for more than a million dollars. His

Canadian Bound, a son of Secretariat, breaks the seven-figure barrier in 1976.

pursuers included Will Farish, a Thoroughbred industry leader and the founder of the posh Lane's End Farm, the renowned Australian trainer Bart Cummings, and Oregon lumberman Aaron U. Jones.

The bidding opened at $500,000 and within ten seconds, the high offer on the gleaming colt soared to $716,000, setting a world record. Only thirty seconds into the battle, the price reached $1 million. Finally, when auctioneer Tom Caldwell's hammer fell at $1.5 million, the yearling's new owner was a six-man Canadian syndicate made up of brothers Jack, Joe, and Ted Burnett; their business associate Henry Federer; Hill n' Dale Farm owner John Sikura; and Toronto dentist Harold Potash. They named their big-ticket acquisition, fittingly, Canadian Bound.

Among the other prominent buyers at that year's Keeneland sale were European soccer pools magnate Robert Sangster, who said he and his associates, Tim Vigors, legendary Irish trainer Vincent O'Brien, and John Magnier, were looking for colts to buy as stallion prospects for their Coolmore-Castle Hyde Stud in Ireland. Their passion for well-bred yearlings, particularly the male offspring of the stout little Canadian Horse of the Year, American champion, and classic winner Northern Dancer, would help fuel an unprecedented upswing in the Thoroughbred marketplace.

Britain's Robert Sangster, center, who helped internationalize the yearling sales, is surrounded by the media after a purchase.

Sangster and his buying team were major players in the Roaring '80s at Keeneland. But, they weren't the only ones willing to spend large fortunes in their quest to own the cream of the North American yearling crop. Sheikh Mohammed bin Rashid Al Maktoum and his three brothers from the Middle Eastern emirate of Dubai were eager to buy top prospects as was former Quarter Horse trainer and future Hall of Famer D. Wayne Lukas, whose emphasis on conformation was attracting a host of wealthy clients.

Sheikh Mohammed would eventually become the ruler of Dubai, but when he first became prominent in the Keeneland market, he was the emirate's Minister of Defense. In the hierarchy of July yearling buyers, however, Sangster and his growing list of investors

were the kings. They fought off Sheikh Mohammed at $3.5 million in 1981 and $4.25 million in 1982.

When Sangster arrived at the Keeneland summer sale of 1983, he had at least twenty principles, agents, relatives, and followers with him, and the prize they had their eyes on was Crescent Farm's Northern Dancer—My Bupers colt, the same yearling Sheikh Mohammed and his entourage also desired most of all.

Late in the evening of a hot July night, they all gathered in the back of the Keeneland sale pavilion and engaged in a ferocious clash, the likes of which had never been seen before at a Thoroughbred auction. According to *The Blood-Horse*, Robert Acton, the manager of Sheikh Mohammed's Aston Upthorpe Stud, "exchanged glances with a member of the Sangster group,

A covered walking ring is one of the recent improvements to the sales facilities.

then said in a matter-of-fact voice: 'There's no use in your bidding, actually. We're going to get the colt.' "

Lukas made a valiant effort with an opening offer of $1 million and kept fighting until the price was just above $5 million. But Sangster wasn't even close to giving up and neither was Sheikh Mohammed. Onward they battled, and eventually Keeneland had to recycle its seven-figure bidding board back to zero to accommodate Sangster's $10-million bid.

When Colonel Richard Warden, Sheikh Mohammed's chief bloodstock adviser, pushed price to $10.2 million, Sangster tried to rally his troops for one more try, suggesting that $10.5 million would be enough to win.

But, *The Blood-Horse* reported, Phonzie O'Brien, a member of Sangster's team, disagreed.

"It doesn't make any difference. They're not going to quit," he said. "We're going to lose."

Sangster backed down, and Sheikh Mohammed ascended to Keeneland's buying throne

with the world's first eight-figure Thoroughbred yearling. The colt, named Snaafi Dancer, didn't hold his world mark long, nor did he amount to anything as a racehorse. Seattle Dancer shattered the world record only two years later with his even more astounding $13.1-million price.

Lukas, accompanied by L.R. French, Mel Hatley, and Eugene Klein, had plenty of financial firepower, and it was more than enough to surpass the old world record of $10.2 million, but it had a limit: $13 million. Sangster's syndicate, led by Coolmore Stud, Niarchos, and Danny Schwartz of Los Angeles, was able to squeeze out one more bid and ended up with a strapping colt that developed into a group II winner in Ireland.

It was a heady time in the Thoroughbred industry, and consignors were entertaining shoppers at lavish parties. An article published in *Town & Country* reported that Tom Gentry hosted a carnival-style bash with a merry-go-round, a Ferris wheel, camel and elephant rides, and a performance by Burt Bacharach; Hunt served a buffet dinner featuring Texas cuisine; and Leslie Combs II held a blowout at his Spendthrift Farm that included cocktails by the pool, salmon and beef served under three white tents, and entertainment by KC and the Sunshine Band.

But the good times didn't continue to roll. Thoroughbred owners lost the tax breaks that had made investments in horses so appealing, and the marketplace at Keeneland and elsewhere went into a severe slump. Meanwhile, the tastes of buyers and sellers at Keeneland were in transition, as were the fortunes of two of the auction firm's sales.

The summer yearling auction started losing some of its luster as the Thoroughbred industry's fanciest venue while the September yearling sale gained strength. Keeneland had started offering yearlings in September in 1950 after selling them at various other times in the fall. Over the

years, the auction became known as a place where consignors offered their bread-and-butter horses and buyers could choose from a wide variety of yearlings at reasonable prices.

Consignors usually sold their very-best-bred stock in September only when an injury or illness prevented them from being offered in the summer. In 1987 the Keeneland September auction had its first seven-figure horse, the $1.1-million Brush Aside. Sheikh Mohammed and his family's Darley Stud Management purchased the son of Alleged from Farish's Lane's End.

At the time, the price seemed like an anomaly, but gradually consignors started seeing the advantage of offering their top yearlings later in the year, giving them more time to mature and be at their peak physically. The September auction, which began offering select sessions to showcase consignors' best-bred and -conformed stock in 1989, produced two seven-figure yearlings for the first time in 1997, and in 2000 twenty-eight September yearlings commanded prices of $1 million or more.

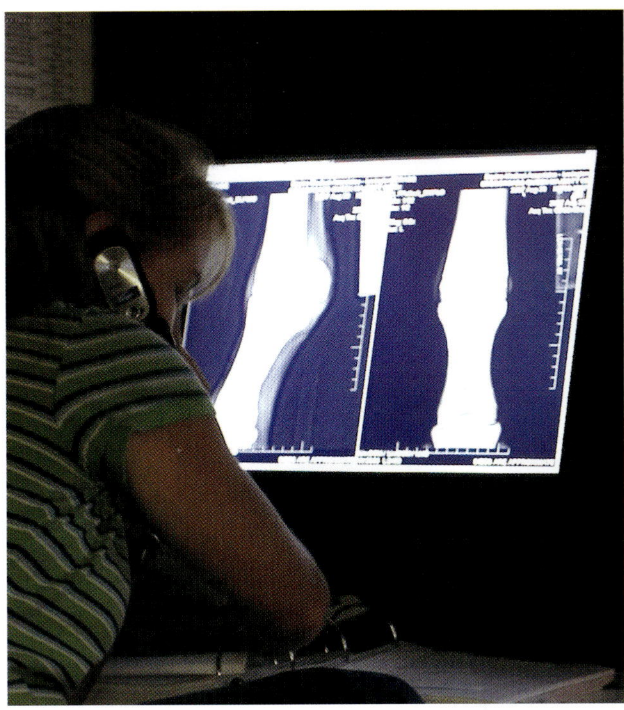

Keeneland was the first auction company to introduce a repository for medical records and X-rays.

The late twentieth century also brought another change to Keeneland when its leaders decided to start selling two-year-olds in training. The first juvenile auction was held in April 1993, grossing $6,817,500 in its first edition. The total had more than doubled by 1996, and it grew to $18,560,000 in 1999. In 2003 it increased to more than $20 million.

In the mid-1990s Keeneland upgraded its auction facilities by adding a repository, where buyers' veterinarians could view X-rays and endoscopic exam videos of young horses. The information there, the veterinarians said, helped them give better advice to their clients, and some consignors found it reduced the number of veterinary exams their horses had to undergo.

In 2003 Keeneland officials canceled the July yearling sale, as the summer auction had come to be known, citing a downturn in the American economy and a sharp reduction in the Kentucky foal crop of 2002 because of mare reproductive loss syndrome. In 2004 Keeneland's executives discontinued the July sale indefinitely, saying "the market dictated it preferred one yearling sale annually at Keeneland, that being in September."

Time marches on, and the business of selling horses at Keeneland keeps apace; opposite, sales participants take a breather in a room in the sales pavilion named for Northern Dancer; below, renovations and upgrades take place between sales.

The Keeneland September sale is the company's only auction ever to have a session postponed. But the interruption was brief, lasting only a day. It happened on September 11, 2001. The morning of the sale's second day began quietly, but soon people were gathered around television monitors in the barn area and the sale pavilion, watching horrifying images of a burning World Trade Center and a smoking Pentagon in the wake of terrorist attacks.

Keeneland officials decided to delay the start of selling by an hour. Then, after the disturbing developments continued to mount, they postponed the session until the following day and moved back the rest of the auction accordingly.

"It's more about humanity than it is business," Keeneland president

Nick Nicholson said at the time. "We didn't enjoy making the decision, but we think it is the right thing to do. It wasn't appropriate to have a horse sale on a day when so many people have suffered."

When the auction resumed the next day, the mood was grim, but that September sale ended up being the second strongest on record.

"We think this was a cowardly act against civilians, and we are 100 percent against it," Sheikh Mohammed told reporters the morning of September 12. "We are 100 percent with America, and we will do anything we can to get these people, to get justice. We shouldn't stop with our lives and let them gain anything."

In 2005 Keeneland unveiled a newly renovated auction pavilion at its September sale. The improvements included an expansion totaling 17,000 square feet, high-speed wireless Internet access, more than seventy flat-panel televisions, a state-of-the-art digital sound and graphics system, new conference rooms, and a larger business center.

In 2006 the September sale upped the Thoroughbred world auction record for

A broodmare is led back to the barn after going through the auction ring.

Buyers examine sales prospects back at the barns; above, Playful Act sets a record price of $10.5 million at the 2007 November breeding stock sale.

gross revenue for the third consecutive year, raising the amount to $399,791,800. The number of horses sold, 3,556, also was believed to be a world mark, and it would grow to 3,799 the following year. In addition, the 2006 September auction's average, $112,427, and median, $45,000, both were sale records as was the $11.7-million price brought by Meydan City, a Kingmambo—Crown of Crimson colt.

Bidding battles between Sheikh Mohammed and Coolmore Stud's Magnier helped pump up the September numbers. But so did Keeneland's efforts to attract buyers from emerging markets in such countries as Mexico, Argentina, Australia, Russia, South Korea, Turkey, and the Philippines.

The sales' increasingly international focus in the twenty-first century has resulted in the selling of Thoroughbreds to nearly fifty countries around the globe and with an increasing percentage of total foreign sales coming from emerging markets. This emerging markets program is led by director of sales Geoffrey Russell, sales marketing associate Chauncey Morris, associate director of sales Thomas Thornbury, and director of racing Rogers Beasley.

The sales team travels to foreign markets on a regular basis to find new buyers, build international relationships, and promote the improvement of Thoroughbred racing around the world. Keeneland has also been successful in helping countries improve their racing and breeding programs through seminars and development of their own sales.

Another growth spurt in the new century took place at Keeneland's 2007 November auction, which generated its highest ever gross of $340,877,200 ($340,727,200 according to *The Blood-Horse*), and was the fourth-highest grossing sale in Thoroughbred auction history. Playful Act established what then was a world mark for a broodmare sold at public auction with her price of $10.5 million.

The worst financial crisis since the 1930s and a global economic setback sent Thoroughbred auction prices spiraling downward during the beginning of the fall 2008 and again in 2009, but Keeneland remained a dominant force in the commercial

Northern Dancer and His Legacy

Northern Dancer is considered perhaps the greatest Thoroughbred sire of the twentieth century. Bred by Canadian industrialist E.P. Taylor, the diminutive Northern Dancer did not find a buyer as a yearling, failing to meet his reserve of $25,000. He joined Taylor's Windfields Farm racing stable, where he proved one of the best buy-backs of all time.

A Canadian champion at two, Northern Dancer excelled at three when he won the 1964 Flamingo Stakes, Florida Derby, the Kentucky Derby, and the Preakness Stakes.

During his stud career, the bay son of Nearctic was represented by 147 stakes winners, including numerous champions on four continents. His influence on Keeneland's yearling sales was unmatched. At the July selected yearling sale Northern Dancer ranked as the leading sire by average 12 times, from 1974-1988, highlighted by the 1984 sale where his twelve yearlings sold for a record average of $3.4 million each. Acknowledged as perhaps the greatest "sire of sires," Northern Dancer's dominance continues through such sons and grandsons as Danzig, Storm Cat, and others whose offspring routinely top the Keeneland sales.

Thoroughbred business. With its up-to-date sale pavilion and its innovative approach to technological advances such as digital X-rays and online marketing, Keeneland is poised to make the most of the next period of growth in the Thoroughbred selling cycle.

Keeneland's founders

Articles of incorporation are filed for Keeneland Association on April 17. Hal Price Headley is elected president of Keeneland Association; Jack Young, first vice president; A.B. Gay, second vice president; Brownell Combs, secretary; and W.H. Courtney, treasurer. Headley would serve as Keeneland Association president from 1935-1951 … On August 29 Keeneland Association purchases 147½ acres of Fayette County sportsman J.O. "Jack" Keene's property on the Versailles Pike for $130,000 in cash and $10,000 in preferred stock at par value.

1936

More than 15,000 people attend an open house at the racetrack on October 11, held primarily to introduce the public to the new totalizator, the first to be installed in Kentucky … An agreement is ratified with Turf Catering Company of Chicago for the operation of all concessions … On October 15 the gates officially open for the first race meeting of the Keeneland Association. All is in readiness, with the clubhouse, grandstand, and grounds completed in good order. For the meeting, honorary stewards are appointed and serve on a rotating

basis. They are Major Beard, Roy Carruthers, Brownell Combs, Richard Deupree, A. B. Hancock Sr., W. Arnold Hanger, J. O. Keene, Henry Knight, Charles Middleton, Charles Nuckols Sr., Thomas Piatt, and Barry Shannon. Steward for the association is C. J. Fitzgerald Jr. Racing secretary is Charles G. McLennan … Royal Raiment, a two-year-old gray filly owned by John Hay Whitney, is Keeneland's inaugural winner. Paid attendance for the nine-day fall meeting (October 15-24) totals 25,337 … December 31 financial statement for the year reveals a net loss of $3.47 … Note: For the following year, 1937, and for every year thereafter (excluding the war years 1943-1945) the Keeneland Association will conduct two race meetings per year, in spring and fall.

From the start racing is a success

1937

Keeneland's first spring meeting features four stakes races, three of which, the Blue Grass Stakes, Ben Ali Handicap, and Phoenix Handicap, were stakes features of the old Kentucky Association meetings. The fourth, the Lafayette Stakes, sees its inaugural running at this meeting. On April 20, Keeneland stages a showing of seven outstanding geldings retired from racing — Sarazen, Mike Hall, Osmand, Clyde Van Dusen, Jolly Roger, Cherry Pie, and Merrick … The association renews the four stakes races from the inaugural fall meeting — the Ashland, Keen, Lexington, and the Breeders' — with three of the four races being dropped after this running … The year-end financial report shows an $8,000 net profit from the first full year of racing.

1938

On April 25 the first auction of Thoroughbreds is held in the Keeneland paddock. A total of thirty-one lots brings $24,885, an average of $802.74. High price of $3,500 is given by F. F. Woodward for Marmitina, a nine-year-old mare by Light Brigade with a suckling colt at

Jockeys in the early days

her side … In addition to the spring and fall meetings, held in eleven and ten days, respectively, Keeneland hosts two Thoroughbred Club of America yearling judging contests, one for colts and one for fillies. Winners are Greentree Farms' chestnut colt by Equipoise-Goose Egg and John Hay Whitney's bay filly by Pharamond II-Blue Dust.

1939

Purse minimum is raised to $700 from the $600 set in 1936 … The track's stall capacity is increased to 530 with the completion of a new thirty-two-stall barn … W. Arnold Hanger presents to Keeneland the 2,300-volume library of Robert Turnbull, collector of equine literature. This gift marks the beginning of the present Keeneland Library, one of the most comprehensive turf libraries in the world.

1940

The Keeneland Association charter is amended to form the association into a holding company rather than an operating company. The association begins to lease its property to the new operating company, Keeneland Race Course. All association income, less expenses, is to be distributed to tax-exempt organizations … The Ashland Stakes renews as a six-furlong race for three-year-old fillies … Keeneland introduces the electric starting gate … Calumet Farm's great Whirlaway wins the Breeders' Futurity … Louis Lee Haggin II is elected Keeneland Race Course president, a position he holds until 1956.

Haggin

1941

Trainer E. L. Cotton and jockey Albert Bodiou combine to win the Phoenix Handicap with Cherry Jam and the Ben Ali with Red Dock, both for Greentree Stables … Woodvale Farms' Our Boots easily beats Calumet's Whirlaway in the Blue Grass Stakes. Whirlaway goes on to win the Triple Crown … The Thoroughbred Club of America Dinner Purse has its inaugural running … Ben Jones, Calumet Farm's trainer, saddles twelve winners during the spring meeting, setting a Keeneland record.

Standing room only

1942

The outbreak of war calls away many race goers and track employees, including W. T. Bishop, general manager … Savage Sailor wins the fourth race on April 14, and pays $212.20, a

Keeneland's first tent sale

Keeneland record. Shut Out with Eddie Arcaro in the saddle wins the Blue Grass by 3½ lengths then goes on to win the Kentucky Derby … All net profits from the fall meeting are earmarked to help with the war effort and $35,000 is given to the Lexington War Chest … Keeneland patrons buy over $27,000 in war bonds and stamps … The fall meeting is the last held at Keeneland until 1946.

1943

Keeneland is classified as a suburban plant and is requested not to operate because of war shortages, specifically the shortage of gasoline and rubber (saving gas and wear on tires by not driving long distances) … Keeneland leases Churchill Downs, where streetcars can drop off patrons, for the ten-day spring meeting … On May 27, Jack Keene, namesake for Keeneland Race Course, collapses at the Fair Grounds racetrack in Detroit and dies later that day … The first yearling sale at Keeneland is conducted by Fasig-Tipton under a tent in the paddock. The auction runs for three days (August 9-11). Hoop Jr., one of the first crop of yearlings sold, will win the Kentucky Derby two years later … The Breeders' Futurity is held as part of the fall meeting at Churchill Downs, as it is for 1944 and 1945.

1944

Spring meeting is held at Churchill Downs, April 15-22. Racing during this week is held for charity … Keeneland Association leases grounds and facilities to the newly organized Breeders' Sales Company … Breeders' Sales Company conducts its first summer yearling sale, with 437 horses sold for $2,285,947, establishing a new record total for a yearling sale … On December 1 the Keeneland Foundation is organized and incorporated for the purpose of promoting scientific research. The foundation receives an initial grant of $47,500 from the association.

1945

Nine-day spring meeting is held in mid-May at Churchill Downs after the Office of War Mobilization lifts a five-month ban on racing ... The Lafayette Stakes is not renewed in this year ... The Blue Grass Stakes is held in June as part of Churchill Downs' race meeting.

1946

With the war over, Keeneland moves into a new era of growth and enthusiasm ... The spring meeting features photo-finish equipment for the first time ... Spring meeting sets Keeneland records for attendance (79,521) and mutuel handle ($3,369,253) ... The Breeders' Sales Company establishes a record gross on the sale of 415 horses, $4,113,480 ... The fall records are broken, with 55,752 in attendance and a handle of $2,482,679.

1947

A record handle is realized during the spring meeting, $3,594,738 ... Ben Jones and jockey Doug Dodson combine to win the Blue Grass Stakes with Faultless and the Ben Ali Handicap with Pot O'Luck, both for Calumet Farm ... In June the Keeneland Foundation donates an electron microscope to the University of Kentucky ... The fall meeting sets records, with attendance at 65,217 and a handle of $2,829,700. For the second successive fall meeting jockey Steve Brooks leads all riders with seventeen wins.

1948

A violent windstorm hits Keeneland just before the spring meeting, killing a groom, injuring others, and heavily damaging two barns ... Calumet Farm comes close to sweeping the spring stakes races, winning the Blue Grass Stakes with Coaltown, the Phoenix Handicap with Coaltown, the Ben Ali Handicap with Fervent, and the Ashland Stakes with Bewitch ... Keeneland purchases additional land to accommodate a seven-furlong chute, an extension to the Headley course, and additional parking.

First equine air transort

1949

Keeneland installs an inside aluminum rail for its spring meeting, replacing the conventional wooden rail. The new rail, at a cost of approximately $5,000, is the first of its kind to be used at an American racetrack. The Blue Grass Stakes added purse is raised to $20,000 from $15,000 ... Woody Stephens

saddles both the Blue Grass and the Ashland Stakes winners for Woodvale Farm ... A one-day attendance record is set on April 23 with 16,229 present ... Oil Capitol, Tom Gray's two-year-old colt, wins two stakes races and sets a new Keeneland earnings record with $47,116, and a new stable "First money won" record, besting the old mark by $5,000.

A well-dressed crowd

1950

Keeneland board of directors approves the purchase of twenty-six additional acres ... The spring meeting features a new box seat area, the old wooden structure replaced by concrete and aluminum ... The racing colors of C.V. Whitney dominate the spring meeting, taking the Blue Grass Stakes, the Phoenix, and the Ben Ali ... Keeneland renews the two-year Breeders' Sales Company lease.

1951

For the first time, both the Blue Grass Stakes and the Lafayette Stakes are run in two divisions ... Guy Huguelet succeeds charter president and director Hal Price Headley as president of the Association, a position he holds through 1955 ... For the second spring in a row Ken Church leads all riders with nine wins and C. V. Whitney is the leading money-winning owner.

1952

Eddie Arcaro rides Hill Gail to victory in the Phoenix, setting the stage for a Derby win. Lafayette Stakes runs in two divisions again. Spring meeting mutuel handle tops $4 million for the first time ... Keeneland repays the last of the money borrowed in 1935 to finance the track ... The fall meeting sets a new mutuel record, topping $3 million for the first time. The Alcibiades is inaugurated for two-year-old fillies.

C. V. Whitney

Nashua in 1956

After the spring meeting, work begins on the enlargement of the grandstand. This work is completed in time for the fall meeting and adds 1,542 seats and increases the structure's capacity — including boxes — to 3,849. A new feature of the grandstand is a dining room with a capacity of 384. Also, the finish line is moved 184 feet closer to the first turn. Moving the finish line lengthens the stretch run from 990 to 1,174 feet, and the Headley Course, formerly forty feet shorter than a half-mile, is increased to four furlongs and 152 feet. In addition, the new finish line made possible the Beard Course of seven furlongs and 184 feet. Records are set in attendance and handle for the fall meeting, owing to the new seats … 75,856 patrons wager $3,777,318 over the twelve-day meeting … Hal Price Headley disperses broodmares at the Breeders' Sales Company fall sale, netting $672,400 for thirty-four mares. A grant of $200,000 is made by the foundation to build Keeneland Hall at the University of Kentucky.

A film patrol system is in use at the spring meeting for the first time … Dr. J. G. Catlett is the first appointee under a new policy of accepting a steward appointed by The Jockey Club … On May 14 work begins on a new 5/8-mile training track and will continue for more than a year. Records are set at the Keeneland summer yearling sale, with a Walnut Springs Farm colt selling for an American record price of $86,000, and the sales average reaches $9,940 … Masaka, a mare from the Aga Khan consignment at the November breeding stock auction, brings a record $105,000 from John S. Phipps.

Keeneland offers $10,000 to furnish Salk anti-polio vaccine for Fayette County preschool-aged children whose families cannot afford to pay to have their children inoculated … Keeneland president Guy Huguelet dies in late July … In September the training track opens … Hasty House Farms wins its sixth stakes race and becomes the first stable to win a Keeneland gold tray. Sea O'Erin is the star horse, winning the Phoenix and the Ben Ali … Steve Brooks wins five races in an eight-race program, setting a record matched only four other times in fifty years … Bwamazon Farm's Jovial Jove wins the Breeders' Futurity.

At the Breeders' Sales Company January sale, Stavros Niarchos buys Segula, dam of Nashua, for $126,000, the highest price to date for a broodmare at public auction … Louis Lee Haggin II is elected Keeneland Association president, a position he holds until 1970. Duval A. Headley is elected Keeneland Race Course president … Between the spring and fall meetings, the main track is completely overhauled at a cost of $150,000 … Leslie Combs II sells a filly for a record $63,000 at the summer sale … On October 18, Nashua, the 1955 Horse of the Year, gallops at Keeneland in his final public appearance prior to going to stud at Spendthrift Farm. The $50,000-added Spinster is inaugurated on October 19. Claiborne Farm sets a record for most money won at a single meeting — $93,589.

Claiborne Farm wins the Phoenix Handicap with Bandit and a Keeneland gold tray for winning six gold julep cups … A record high average is set at the summer sale, $11,789 for 235 horses … The fall race meeting and the Breeders' Sale Company fall sale are held concurrently … The first thirteen-day race meeting yields a record fall meeting mutuel handle of over $4 million.

At its spring meeting, Keeneland holds daily double wagering and an eight-race card for the first time in its history … Twenty-five additional acres purchased form adjoining holdings … In September Keeneland hosts the Southern Governor's Conference for the city of Lexington … 89,023 patrons wager a record $5,238,579 at the fall meeting, which for the first time includes three Saturday race days … A 4 percent parimutuel tax is re-imposed by the state … J. Graham Brown's Bornastar is the leading money-winning horse for the second year in a row.

The daily double is a hit

1959

Fred Turner Jr.'s Tomy Lee sets up his Kentucky Derby win with a victory in the Blue Grass Stakes over Claiborne's Dunce ... Tomy Lee is the leading money-winning horse for the spring meeting ... Spring mutuels set a record, $4,891,872 ... Autumn meeting introduces Monday racing for the first time since 1937 ... Allan "Doc" Lavin succeeds the late Fred Burton as racing secretary and handicapper ... Hal Price Headley wins his 100th race at Keeneland with Rash Statement in the Alcibiades ... The Fayette Handicap is inaugurated.

1960

The spring meeting is increased to thirteen days. The C.V. Whitney stable leads all owners and trainers in wins and money won, with eight and $43,540, respectively. For the first time, there is a seven-way tie for leading trainer. For the ninth time, jockey Steve Brooks leads all riders in wins with eighteen ... In May the board of trustees of the Keeneland Foundation dissolve the foundation and distribute $102,146.12 (the last of its assets) to the University of Kentucky to provide a perpetual scholarship in agriculture ... Owners, trainers, and jockeys with 25 wins or more are honored at the silver anniversary dinner party. All-time leaders are owner Hal Price Headley, trainer V. R. Wright, and jockey Steve Brooks.

1961

The spring meeting brings the introduction of the alphanumeric message board located at ground level in front of the infield tote board. T. A. Grissom's Eight Again wins the Phoenix in record-matching time. Mary Fisher's Goldflower beats a good field to win the Ashland ... A record price is paid for a yearling at auction, $130,000 from John M. Olin ... During the fall meeting, Keeneland becomes the first Thoroughbred track in America to use the Visumatic Timer (which posts the various fractions and final clocking on the tote board) ... Three new track records are set at the fall meeting ... Jockey Willie Carstens wins the Lafayette on Crimson Satan and the Alcibiades on Journalette — the only stakes races he will ever win at Keeneland.

1962

A proposal to merge the Breeders' Sales Company and Keeneland Association is introduced at Breeders' Sales' annual meeting; Keeneland Association takes over the business of selling horses ... Hal Price Headley dies of a heart attack at Keeneland March 22 ... Ridan wins the Blue Grass Stakes by four lengths over eventual Derby winner Decidedly and a strong field ... An ambitious three-part building program is revealed in December. The goal is to double seating capacity for the grandstand and the dining facilities.

1963

The spring meeting marks the return of 1 1/16-mile races, which had not been run at Keeneland since the finish line was relocated in the fall of 1953. An alternate finish line is installed at the sixteenth pole ... Decidedly, the 1962 Derby winner, scores the second stakes win of his career in the Ben Ali in track-record time. Cain Hoy Stable's Sally Ship beats undefeated Bonnie's Girl by a nose in the Ashland. Editorialist repeats his 1962 win in the Phoenix. Eventual Derby winner Chateaugay from Darby Dan Farm wins the Blue Grass Stakes over a game Get Around ... Major construction work in the linking of the grandstand and clubhouse is complete before the fall meeting ... Keeneland president L. L. Haggin's Choker wins the Fayette Handicap.

1964

Headley Course chute is extended from 4 furlongs, 152 feet to 4 1/2 furlongs. Blue Norther equals stakes record time in winning the Ashland ... Choker, winner of the Phoenix, also wins the Ben Ali but is put back to second. Bill Hartack eases Northern Dancer to a half-length win in the Blue Grass Stakes ... Keeneland presents gold julep cups to leading sales consignors ... Autumn meeting sets attendance record with 80,534 for eleven days ... Old Hat, under Don Brumfield, wins the Spinster ... Leslie Combs II ends his sixteen-year run of maintaining the highest sales average for the July select sale.

Northern Dancer winning the Blue Grass Stakes

1965

L. L. Haggin returns for his 10th successive term as Keeneland president ... J. Graham Brown's Gallant Romeo wins the Phoenix, giving the Louisville hotelman his sixth stakes win and a Keeneland gold tray. Kelso, five time Horse of the Year (1960-1964), appears at Keeneland the day before the Blue Grass Stakes as part of his tour of American tracks.

Proceeds from his appearances are used for equine research. Lucky Debonair, the Vertex colt of Mrs. Ada Rice, wins the Blue Grass by a half-length, then goes on to win the Derby ... First $5 million sales plateau reached at the summer sale, with a record $17,973 average. Foreign purchases at all of Keeneland's sales in 1965 go over the million-dollar mark ($1,019,725) for the first time in history ... A. B. Hancock's unbeaten Moccasin wins the Alcibiades.

1966

Graustark, the early Derby favorite, romps through two winning races at Keeneland but then is beaten on a sloppy track by Abe's Hope in the Blue Grass. Graustark is found to have broken a coffin bone and is out for the Derby. Swift Ruler, loser in 1965 to Lucky Debonair in the Blue Grass, returns to Keeneland to win the Ben Ali Handicap ... Keeneland announces plans to build its long-awaited new sales arena, replacing the 1929 structure that was moved to Keeneland from its Paris Pike location in 1944 ... New sales volume record set at $5,906,400 at the fall sale of breeding stock.

1967

Twenty closed-circuit TV monitors, without audio, are placed in grandstand and clubhouse locations ... Moccasin wins the Phoenix Handicap for A. B. Hancock Jr. after a disappointing three-year-old season. Florida-bred Diplomat Way wins the Blue Grass Stakes after the withdrawal of fellow Floridian and favorite Dr. Fager ... Frank McMahon pays $250,000, a world record, for a son of Raise A Native at the summer sale ... TV Commercial returns to Keeneland to win the Breeders' Futurity for Bwamazon Farm. Swoonaway wins the Fayette Handicap on closing day.

1968

Plans are approved for a new sales pavilion ... James E. "Ted" Bassett III is named assistant to association president Louis Lee Haggin II ... Spring meeting sets records for attendance (9,240 daily) and mutuel handle ($7,871,443). Calumet wins its fifth Blue Grass Stakes with Forward Pass ... Main track is renovated over the summer ... A record price of $405,000 is paid for a yearling at the summer sale ... Fall meeting lasts nineteen days, the longest in track history. Claiborne Farm is the first stable to win the Keeneland gold pitcher, signifying twelve stakes wins.

1969

The fifteen-day spring meeting is the longest in history and produces a record mutuel handle, $8,339,842 ... Keeneland hosts the Republican Governor's Conference, chaired by California Governor Ronald Reagan ... New $700,000 sales

Ted Bassett and California Governor Ron Reagan

pavilion is completed on the site of the old one; buyers attending the summer yearling sale enjoy the atmosphere in the new pavilion with its 650 theater-style seats. A sales gross record is set at $7,684,000 ... The fall breeding stock sale grosses a record $11,088,700 ... A new one-day attendance record of 16,412 is set in the fall.

1970

Dust Commander becomes the seventh Blue Grass Stakes winner also to win the Kentucky Derby ... A new photo-finish facility is installed ... Fifty-two additional acres are added, bringing land holdings to 306 acres ... L. L. Haggin is named chairman of the board and Ted Bassett becomes president of the association ... A world-record yearling price, $510,000, is paid for a full brother to Majestic Prince.

1971

Keeneland celebrates its thirty-fifth anniversary ... The five sales during the year generate $28 million in gross receipts ... The Blue Grass Stakes marks the first million-dollar day of wagering in Keeneland's history — $1,052,866. Spring meeting sets records for one-day attendance (18,882) season attendance (138,910), and season handle ($8,848,829) ... Fall meeting sets one-day attendance mark at 16,585, season attendance mark at 110,667, and total mutuel handle of $8,774,474.

1972

Keeneland raises the Blue Grass Stakes to $40,000 added. There are a record 139 nominations for the race ... More closed circuit TV monitors are added for race goers ... Despite bad spring weather, a mutuel record is set at $9,672,256 ... Jockey Don Brumfield rides twenty-four winners in fifteen days ... Summer yearling sale sets a record at $12,070,700.

1973

Howard Battle succeeds "Doc" Lavin as racing secretary and handicapper … The Blue Grass Stakes is increased to $50,000 added. A one-race wagering record, $269,679, is set in the spring … 61-to-1 Raging Whirl wins the Ashland Stakes … Claiborne Farm sets single-consignor record at the summer sale, with eighteen yearlings selling for $2,364,000 … Sales gross for the year (four sales) is $59,423,300. Four forty-stall barns are completed.

1974

Blue Grass Stakes is renewed for fiftieth time (includes 1911-1914 and 1919-1926 at the Kentucky Association track) … The parking lot is expanded, food service stations are added, and portions of the grandstand and clubhouse are renovated … Jockey Don Brumfield wins both divisions of the Ashland Stakes … A spring mutuel record of $11,418,549 is set … World record $625,000 is paid for a yearling at the summer sale … Fall attendance record for one day, 18,814, is realized.

1975

Ashland Stakes is increased to $50,000 added … Tom Caldwell is named director of auctions following the May 10 death of

Tom Caldwell

George Swinebroad … ABC-TV broadcasts the Blue Grass Stakes nationally … $18,344,000 paid for 342 yearlings at the summer sale … Keeneland runs its first $100,000 race — the $130,725 Breeders' Futurity, won by Harbor Springs … Susan's Girl wins the Spinster again … Fall race meet sets a single day attendance record of 21,521.

1976

The Blue Grass Stakes purse is doubled, making it a $100,000-added race. Heavily favored Honest Pleasure captures the Blue Grass and creates a remarkable minus win pool of $41,876.20 … Spring mutuel daily average tops $1 million for the first time … Construction begins on major grandstand renovations … A new section of concrete and steel replaces the historic wooden grandstand that had stood since the track's inaugural meeting … A record 1,009 are entered in the summer sale and the first million dollar horse, Canadian Bound by Secretariat out of Charming Alibi, sells for $1.5 million … The sale sets a new record gross, $71,761,900 … Golden Chance Farm becomes the sixth recipient of the Keeneland gold tray with Run Dusty Run's win in the Breeders' Futurity. A record $12,208,320 is wagered at the fall meeting.

1977

The spring meeting unveils a new press box, jockey's room, grandstand, and clubhouse entrance. The new Lexington Room is introduced … Angel Cordero Jr. wins the Blue Grass and the Spinster … A Keeneland sales graduate, The Minstrel, wins both the Epsom and Irish Sweeps derbies … European buyers push July yearling sale receipts to a world-record $27.6 million with Secretariat's progeny bringing the highest average price for the second (and final) July sale in a row.

1978

Despite rain and cold weather, the spring meeting sets a record attendance with 186,858, with a record betting gross of $16,539,115 … Admiral and Mrs. Gene Markey watch their Alydar run for the first time, in the Blue Grass Stakes, which the colt wins by thirteen lengths … Eddie Delahoussaye becomes fourth jockey to win five races in one day … $1.5 million building program begins, with five thirty-two-stall barns … New infield tote board for fall meeting … $100 million mark topped in 1978 sales.

1979

Two new "Keeneland" hedges are planted, flanking the infield tote board … In the spring Keeneland becomes the first track in Kentucky — and only the fourth in the country — to use the AmTote 300 Series Totalisator System, known as ABC (All Betting and Cashing) Mutuels. This system allows bettors to buy and cash tickets in any amount and type at any window throughout the plant … Spectacular Bid is the sixteenth horse

New Keeneland hedges

to win the Blue Grass Stakes then the Derby … The terrace over the walking ring is enclosed and ready for the fall race meeting … New barns are finished … Keeneland receives over 2,300 entries for November breeding stock sale … Gross sales for Keeneland's four auctions top $150 million, a 33 percent increase over the previous record.

1980

Work begins at the rear of the pavilion on an enclosed walking ring where buyers can inspect horses immediately before they enter the auction ring. The 6,400-square-foot addition is octagonal in shape with a stone facade and floor-length windows. On April 18, Keeneland board chairman Louis Lee Haggin II dies. Single-day attendance record of 22,985 is set during spring meeting … Betting totals a record $16,856,626 … Rockhill Native gives trainer Herb Stevens his first stakes victory at Keeneland … Don Brumfield rides to his 500th win … World-record price of $1.7 million is paid by Niarchos at the July sale … The year's four auctions gross over $232 million. On December 1, William S. Evans retires as Keeneland's director of sales.

1981

The Blue Grass Stakes is raised to $150,000 added … Construction begins on three forty-stall barns on recently purchased property west of the main racetrack with three more barns planned … Two spring meeting Saturday crowds top 22,000 … Robert Sangster smashes the old sales mark for a yearling, paying $3.5 million for a brother of Northernette and Storm Bird … Jockey Julio Espinoza wins both divisions of the Phoenix Breeders' Cup during the fall meet … Sales gross for the year is $319,033,300.

1982

April 2 opening is the earliest in history … A new clubhouse dining room seating 170 people is built overlooking the walking ring … A 3,000-square-foot sales pavilion addition is underway … Constructed of local stone with an exposed wood ceiling, the addition contains a large bar, hot and cold food service counter, a lounge area separated from the room by planters, and eighteen additional telephones … Keeneland sales products Golden Fleece and Touching Wood are 1-2 in Epsom Derby … W. B. Rogers Beasley is named Keeneland's new director of sales … Robert Sangster again sets July yearling sales record, paying $4.25 million for a Nijinsky II colt … Jockey Julio Espinoza wins his fifth Phoenix Breeders' Cup.

Don Brumfield wins 500th race in 1980

Escorted by Ted Bassett, Queen Elizabeth II visitis in 1984

1983

On January 12, longtime Keeneland track superintendent Hobert Burton dies … A second Versailles Road entrance is constructed, providing an additional access lane to Keeneland. Millard Waldheim's Bwamazon Farm becomes the second recipient of a gold pitcher with a win in the Lafayette … Following the spring meeting, Keeneland's training track is renovated … The Fontana Safety Rail is erected on the main track, replacing the inside, aluminum rail installed prior to the 1949 spring meeting … The Lexington Stakes is the newest stakes race for three-year-olds … Improvements for the fall meeting include two new clubhouse ticket booths, a new food service stand and bar on the ground floor of the clubhouse, and additional hard-surface parking … Pat Day is the sixth jockey to ride five winners in one day … A dead heat is declared for the first time in a Keeneland stakes race as Frost King and Cad win the Fayette … New one-day yearling sale set for the day following the July select sale.

1984

The first phase of a $3-million construction project is completed before the spring meeting when sixteen new saddling stalls are built in the paddock during the winter and preliminary work is started on a 40,000-square-foot addition to the rear of the grandstand … Daily attendance record (13,036) and daily mutuel handle record ($1,250,159) are set at spring meeting … Progress is made on the 7 1/2-furlong turf course inside the main track … Thirty-three horses sell for $1 million or more at the Keeneland sales … Completed for the fall meeting, the grandstand addition provides a fine view of the paddock from three levels … Two elevators, located at each end of the addition, connect all floors, and the second and third levels are both enclosed … On October 11, Queen Elizabeth II visits

Keeneland during the fall meeting and presents the trophy for the new Queen Elizabeth II Challenge Cup ... Jockey Don Brumfield wins his sixteenth and final title as leading jockey at Keeneland ... Keeneland pledges $1 million to build the Maxwell A. Gluck Equine Research Center at the University of Kentucky.

1985

A new grandstand entrance adjacent to the paddock and walking ring is ready for the spring meeting ... Keeneland begins a $2.7-million construction project to be completed in early 1986, the year the track celebrates its fiftieth anniversary. The project calls for a 12,000-square-foot addition to Keeneland's administration building that includes a new jockeys' quarters with separate facilities for female jockeys and a new grandstand entrance ... Sales prices go through the roof as a colt (Seattle Dancer) out of Nijinsky II—My Charmer sells for $13.1 million in the July select yearling sale ... Six consignors are honored at Keeneland's annual awards program in April: Windfields Farm (Secreto), Big Sink-Lanes End Associated Farms (Law Society), Windwoods Farm (Tiltalating), Edward L. Stephenson (Triptych), Dave Parrish Jr. (Life's Magic), and Warner L. Jones Jr. (Northern Trick) ... At its fall meeting Keeneland becomes the first organized track in Kentucky to hold grass racing, and offers exacta wagering for the first time in its history. The twenty-seventh Fayette Handicap is taken by longshot Wop Wop on the new turf course.

1986

In March, James E. "Ted" Bassett III is elevated from president to chairman of the board. William C. "Bill" Greely is promoted from vice president to president. Keeneland is designated a National Historic Landmark by the National Park Service ... An addition to the Lexington Room increases its capacity from 250 to almost 500 ... Classy Cathy with jockey Earlie Fires wins the first Beaumont and the fiftieth Ashland Stakes,

Construction in 1984

tying the record time for the Ashland of 1:44 set by Willie Shoemaker aboard Truly Bound in 1981 ... Spring and fall race meetings set records for total attendance, daily average attendance, and mutuel handle ... Owners Edward A. Cox Jr. and Dan Agnew win titles for "most money won" for spring and fall meets respectively ... Keeneland's cumulative community contributions total more than $3,904,102.

Greely

1987

Duval A. Headley, former president of Keeneland Race Course, dies on February 26 ... Terra Incognita with jockey Darrell Foster aboard wins the 1 1/16 mile Alcibiades in a record time of 1:44 3/5. In the Blue Grass Stakes, Alysheba, ridden by Chris McCarron, is disqualified from first and placed third while War, owned by Tom Gentry and trained by D. Wayne Lukas, with jockey Herb McCauley up, is declared victorious ... Alysheba goes on to win the Kentucky Derby and Preakness Stakes ... Sunday Silence, a colt consigned by Arthur Hancock III (as agent for Oak Cliff Thoroughbreds and Thomas P. Tatham), is sold as a yearling at the July sale for $17,000. He goes on to win the Kentucky Derby, Preakness, and Breeders' Cup Classic, and is named Horse of the Year in 1989 ... Race meeting purses top the $5 million mark for the year for the first time.

1988

Fifty-year-old jockey Don Brumfield wins the Ben Ali and Fayette handicaps on Woody Stephens' trained Homebuilder and takes the Forerunner Stakes on Posen. He then goes on to win the Commonwealth Breeders' Cup aboard Calestoga and the Keeneland Breeders' Cup with Niccolo Polo, increasing his total number of stakes victories at Keeneland to thirty-one ... Pick Six wagering is introduced with the opening of the fall race meeting ... Keeneland-sold horses sweep America's Triple Crown for the second year in a row.

1989

The date for the Blue Grass Stakes is changed, moving it to three weeks before the Kentucky Derby ... A stakes race is run each day during the spring meeting, increasing the total to sixteen ... Don Brumfield scores his final Keeneland stakes win in the Beaumont aboard Exquisite Mistress and retires after the spring meet as Keeneland's all-time leading jockey with 716 wins and thirty-two stakes victories ... Trainer Bill Mott, owner Mrs. Bertram Firestone, and jockey Julie Krone team up to win the Bewitch Stakes with Gaily Gaily, setting a track record of 1:50 for 1 1/8 mile on the turf ... D. Wayne Lukas ties with Joe Pierce for leading trainer in the spring with eight wins and goes on to win twenty-two races in the fall race meeting ... A crowd of 28,788 fills the stands on Saturday, October 14 to set a single-day attendance record.

Princess Anne greets Keeneland's jockeys

1990

Go For Wand wins the Ashland and Beaumont Stakes with Randy Romero aboard — he wins thirty-two races during the spring race meeting and ties with Craig Perret to set a new one-day riding record of six wins, both set during the spring race meet … Summer Squall wins the Blue Grass Stakes, places second in the Kentucky Derby, and goes on to win the Preakness. Keeneland offers its first simulcast race, the Arkansas Derby, on April 21 during a live card … Keeneland adds 450 acres with the purchase of adjoining Keene, Murty, and Warrenton farms … Even though the average price is down slightly, the total, $86,499,000, is up for the September yearling sales as 2,913 horses go through the ring. Mutuel handle for on-track and intertrack wagering hits a record $54.7 million with $6.8 million returned in the form of purses … The John Franks dispersal of 659 horses grosses $9,539,100 in the September, November, and January (1991) sales.

1991

Keeneland opens a new gift shop on April 2, called the Paddock Shop, on the ground floor adjacent to the walking ring. A fourth-floor expansion, called the biggest construction project in Keeneland history, including twenty-two corporate boxes and the Phoenix Room, is completed for the spring meeting. The Phoenix Room, with space for 500 people, provides a 220-foot dining area overlooking the walking ring. Keeneland also adds the Lafayette Room (seating for sixty-five) on the fourth floor … Spring meeting features Sunday racing for the first time in Keeneland history. Strike the Gold wins the Blue Grass Stakes and goes on to win the Kentucky Derby … Pat Day wins a record forty-five races in the fall meet, including the first Hopemont Stakes on Stress Buster.

1992

The Blue Grass purse is increased from $350,000 to $500,000 and the race is won by Pistols and Roses with Jacinto Vasquez on top. Rapper M. C. Hammer is in attendance to watch his horse Dance Floor, the odds on favorite in the Blue Grass, finish fourth … The inaugural Doubledogdare Stakes is won by Shane Sellars riding Jeano … Jockey Pat Day on American Chance wins the Lafayette Stakes, tying the record time set by Forty-Niner in 1988 … At the fall meeting Keeneland conducts quinella betting for the first time. Julie Krone becomes the first female jockey to win the Queen Elizabeth II Challenge Cup on Captive Miss … Paul Mellon's Rokeby Stables dispersal at the November sale brings $6,294,600 for thirty-two horses and an average of $196,706.

1993

Keeneland holds its inaugural April two-year-olds in training sale. A total of 108 horses sell for $6,817,500, averaging $63,125, the highest average of any two-year-old sale in North America in 1993 … For the first time in its history, Keeneland proves to be an across-the-board springboard to success in both the Kentucky Derby and Preakness Stakes. The in-the-money finishers in the Derby (Sea Hero, Prairie Bayou, and Wild Gale) and Preakness (Prairie Bayou, Cherokee Run, and El Bakan) all raced at Keeneland's spring meeting. In addition,

Kissin Kris (who was stabled and trained at Keeneland for much of the spring meeting) and Wild Gale (who ran in the Lexington Stakes) finish second and third, respectively, in the Belmont Stakes.

1994

Jockey Mike Smith takes the Blue Grass on Holy Bull ... Keeneland begins full-card simulcasting for the first time in the grandstand on August 20 ... Renowned British mystery writer Dick Francis presents the trophy to the connections of Pharma, including jockey Chris Antley, for the Valley View Breeders' Cup. Julie Krone wins her second Queen Elizabeth II Challenge Cup aboard Irish-bred Danish ... September sales gross, as 2,817 yearlings go through the ring, is $104,709,900 — shattering the previous year's record of $87,710,100. A dispersal of Loblolly Stable horses brings $5,260,000, with an impressive average of $134,872. Mrs. John Hay Whitney's dispersal is equally impressive, grossing $4,115,000 in the July and November sales.

1995

Thunder Gulch, a two-time Keeneland sales graduate, places a disappointing fourth in the Blue Grass Stakes but goes on to win the Kentucky Derby and Belmont Stakes ... For the fall meeting, a new entrance is constructed at the intersection of Versailles Road and Man o' War Boulevard ... Trainer Nick Zito has a very good year at Keeneland, winning three stakes races — the Lafayette, Lexington, and Dowager ... The lady jockeys are also having a great year. Donna Barton wins the Valley View and the Thoroughbred Club of America stakes while Julie Krone takes the Keeneland Breeders' Cup and the Lafayette.

1996

Toyota becomes the sponsor of the Blue Grass Stakes and the purse increases to $700,000. Skip Away, ridden by Shane Sellars, wins the Toyota Blue Grass by six lengths in a time of 1:47 1/5, establishing a new record and upsetting the favorite, Editor's Note, who finishes third ... The Ashland Stakes purse is increased to $500,000-added ... Real Quiet, consigned by Denali Stud, sells for a modest $17,000 in the September yearling sale and will go on to win the Kentucky Derby in 1998. Boston Harbor sweeps a series of two-year-old races at four Kentucky tracks, including the Breeders' Futurity at Keeneland, and earns a $1 million bonus for owner W.T. Young ... For the second year in a row Julie Krone wins the Keeneland Breeders' Cup Mile, this time on Dumaani, a Shadwell Farm horse trained by Kiaran McLaughlin.

1997

Ending a longtime tradition of no public-address system, Keeneland hires Kurt Becker to call the races for the first time

during the spring meeting ... Maker's Mark signs on as the sponsor of the Maker's Mark Mile and begins a tradition of producing limited edition bottles that go on sale opening day of the spring meet with proceeds earmarked for charity — they sell out in a matter of hours ...Total wagering tops $100 million for the first time during the sixteen-day spring meeting ... For the first time in history Keeneland offers drive-through wagering on the Kentucky Derby simulcast. Construction of the Keeneland Entertainment Center is completed on the Keene Farm ... Former President George Bush attends the races as the guest of William Farish, owner of Lane's End farm, and presents the trophy to the owners of Favorite Trick after the undefeated colt romps to victory in the Lane's End Breeders' Futurity. It marks the first time that a former president of the United States has made a trophy presentation at Keeneland ... The 1997 November breeding stock sale sets an industry record for gross sales — $213 million.

1998

Coolmore Stud, the world-famous Irish stallion operation, becomes the sponsor of the Lexington Stakes and the purse is increased to $325,000 ... H.R.H. The Princess Royal, Princess Anne of England attends closing day of the spring meeting to present the trophy in the inaugural running of the Royal Chase for the Sport of Kings, the first steeplechase race ever held at Keeneland. Author Dick Francis is also in attendance ... A $5.8 million renovation of the west end of the grandstand is completed in time for the fall meeting. On the inside, the first and second floors are enclosed, creating an additional 15,200 square feet of climate-controlled space. Storage space on the second floor is converted to public space with mutuel windows, concessions, and restrooms — all accessible via a new escalator. The Sports Bar doubles in size and the Paddock Shop opens a satellite location. Outside, a facade of Kentucky River stone defines the exterior of the west end and

expanded balconies offer patrons a view of the newly landscaped area below ... On October 16 Keeneland hosts the first running of the Vinery First Lady Stakes. The race for fillies and mares is contested at 1 3/16 miles on the Keeneland turf course ... On December 11 the Keeneland Foundation once again files for tax exempt status as a private foundation.

Nicholson

1999

Keeneland president William C. "Bill" Greely announces in September that he will retire in February 2000. George "Nick" Nicholson is selected in November to replace him as the track's sixth president ... Keeneland sales have a record-breaking year. At the July select yearling sale, the average of $581,932 breaks the previous record average established in 1984. The highest gross ever for a yearling sale, $233,020,800, is reached during the September sale, breaking the record previously set at the 1984 July sale … The national unveiling of the Secretariat stamp takes place at Keeneland on October 16 as part of the U.S. Postal Service's "Celebrate the Century" program … The November sale establishes the highest volume in sales history, $317,666,000, breaking the record set at the same sale in 1998. A record 3,461 horses are sold.

2000

On April 24 the Keeneland Foundation is officially granted tax-exempt status by the Internal Revenue Service. It is classified as a 501(c)(3) and will serve as a conduit for the Keeneland Association to provide benefits to the community and industry.

The new covered walking ring

Fran Taylor is named executive director of the foundation … The outdoor first floor of the Keeneland clubhouse undergoes a major renovation in the summer. The area is completely enclosed and renovations include the addition of a slate floor, brick pavers, Keeneland's signature two-over-two stonework, new mutuel windows, concession stands, and more than 100 closed-circuit televisions. The clubhouse renovation is completed for the fall race meeting … Three of the five sales — July ($621,015), September ($88,085), and November ($92,466) — post record averages. Record yearling prices for a colt of $6.8 million and filly of $4.4 million also are set at the September auction as the gross reaches a record $291,827,100 … Keeneland launches the Thoroughbred industry's first Internet auction on September 17. More than 200 buyers and agents register to bid … A 13,000-square-foot covered show ring is unveiled at the 2000 September yearling sale. The show ring is built to provide additional safety for buyers, sellers, and horses as well as provide shelter from inclement weather.

2001

James E. "Ted" Bassett III, chairman of the board since March 1986, announces his retirement in October. He remains a Keeneland trustee … Two Keeneland stakes are upgraded for 2002 — the Shadwell Keeneland Turf Mile, from grade II to grade I, and the Raven Run, from ungraded to grade III. Keeneland now has six grade I stakes races on the flat. During the second session of the Keeneland September yearling sale (postponed one day due to the terrorist attacks in New York City and Washington, D.C.), a Storm Cat colt sells for $6.4 million, the second-highest price in the history of the sale … Keeneland leads a fund drive during the September sales and

raises $5.7 million for 9-11 Relief … During the inaugural October yearling sale, 338 horses bring $5,092,900 for an average of $15,068. Top price is $400,000 for a Pleasant Colony colt … After serving as director of sales for nineteen years, W. B. Rogers Beasley is tapped to be Keeneland's director of racing. Geoffrey Russell is named director of sales.

2002

Howard Battle, Keeneland's longtime racing secretary, dies on July 14. Battle stepped down as racing secretary earlier in the year and assumed the role of stakes coordinator. Ben Huffman is named as his replacement. Keeneland's new 10,000-square-foot library opens to the public on July 15 … Seabiscuit, a feature movie produced by Universal Studios and based on the book by Laura Hillenbrand, begins filming at Keeneland. Parts of Keeneland, including the infield, track, grandstand, clubhouse, and lawn, are retrofitted to look like Pimlico Race Course circa 1938. On November 17, more than 4,000 unpaid extras turn out to be a part of the match race between Seabiscuit and War Admiral … George "Bucky" Sallee, Keeneland's longtime hornblower, marks his 10,000th call to the post on October 9.

2003

Citing the effects of Mare Reproductive Loss Syndrome, Keeneland officials place the July select yearling sales on hiatus. During the spring, William Farish is presented with a gold pitcher for his 12th stakes on the same day that Princess Anne enjoys her second visit to Keeneland … The Lane's End Breeders' Futurity, a 1 1/16-mile race for two-year-olds, is elevated to grade I and the Raven Run, a seven-furlong sprint for three-year-old fillies, is upgraded to grade II … The seventeen-day October race meeting establishes an on-track attendance record of 232,499. Claiborne Farm becomes the first owner to win the Keeneland gold bowl when Yell wins the Raven Run Stakes … Breeders' Cup Juvenile Fillies winner Cash Run, in foal to Storm Cat, ties a world-record price for a broodmare sold at public auction

Claiborne Farm's golden bowl

when Coolmore's John Magnier pays $7.1 million for her at the November breeding stock sale ... Keeneland's longtime racing secretary Howard Battle receives a posthumous Eclipse Award of Merit. The Keeneland Library receives a Special Eclipse Award.

2004

Expansion and renovation of Keeneland's sales pavilion begins and is scheduled for completion in August 2005. The expansion includes a 5,000-square-foot space for the repository, more and larger conference rooms, and a kitchen to service the dining areas. Enhancements include hi-speed wireless Internet access throughout the facility, a new business center, an upgraded sound system, and a larger press box ... During the April meet, the record books are rewritten for total, daily average, and single-day attendance figures in addition to record all-source total and daily average and on-track total and daily average mutuel handles ... Sale records for highest-priced horses are set during the April two-year-old and September yearling sales. During the April sale a Pulpit colt sells for $3.3 million and records are set for gross revenues ($22,012,000), average price ($217,941), and median ($135,000). A Storm Cat colt sells for $8 million in September as the sale sets records for number of horses sold (3,370), average ($96,411), median ($37,000), and gross ($324,904,300) on its way to becoming the biggest sale in history ... Installation of Polytrack, a synthetic surface, is completed in September on the 5/8-mile training track. It is the first of its type at a public racing or training facility in North America. Evidence indicates that Polytrack is safer for horses and riders and requires less maintenance ... At the November sale, a record average is established ($97,348) and the record for median is equaled ($32,000).

2005

Keeneland's spring meeting posts a record total attendance — 235,220 — and the second highest on-track mutuel handle in history. Included in the total are two of the three largest crowds in track history — a record 33,621 on Toyota Blue Grass Day and 30,110 on Ashland Stakes Day ... Keeneland introduces the ten-cent superfecta wager ... On September 2, longtime Keeneland trustee and board member Charles Nuckols Jr. dies. Later that month, William T. "Buddy" Bishop, a prominent Lexington attorney and longtime board member and secretary of Keeneland, is named trustee ... At the September sale, Keeneland unveils its newly renovated sales pavilion. The September yearling sale concludes as the largest-grossing Thoroughbred auction in the world, with record gains in gross ($384,349,900 for 3,545 horses), average ($108,420), and median ($40,000) prices. Additionally, the number of horses commanding $1 million or more, forty, sets an industry record. At $9.7 million, a record is established when John Ferguson, on behalf of Sheikh Mohammed bin

Rashid al Maktoum, purchases a colt by Storm Cat out of Tranquility Lake ... In October Keeneland's board of directors instruct management to continue the planning, design, and engineering for the installation of Polytrack on its main track during the summer of 2006 ... During the November breeding stock sale, champion female and broodmare prospect Ashado attracts a world record bid of $9 million, the highest price ever paid for a broodmare or broodmare prospect. Records for average price ($102,842) and median price ($35,000) also are established.

2006

Record gross sales of $72,329,100 are established for the January horses of all ages sale ... The spring race meeting posts all-time record wagering and attendance figures. Total wagering of $143,459,422 is an all-time meet record while total wagering averages a record $9,563,961 per day. Attendance for the fifteen-day meet totals a record 244,145, including a single-day attendance record for a Friday of 23,882, set on Good Friday, April 14, which is also Maker's Mark Mile Day. Daily attendance during the meet averages a record 16,276 ... Julien Leparoux becomes the first apprentice jockey to win a leading rider title at Keeneland when he ties with Rafael Bejarano for top honors in the spring meet standings. Leparoux returns to win the title again in the fall, on his way to earning an Eclipse Award as the nation's leading apprentice jockey ... Keeneland

Drainage system for Polytrack

becomes only the third racetrack in North America, joining Turfway Park in Florence, Kentucky, and Woodbine Racetrack in Toronto, to install a Polytrack racing surface on its main track. The track is also reconfigured to widen the turns and lengthen the stretch. Other significant improvements include the installation of a state-of-the-art LED tote board; enlargement of the trackside apron along the grandstand and clubhouse lawn to create additional space for patrons; a larger winner's circle; and construction of a stone and wrought iron trackside rail along the grandstand and clubhouse aprons. Keeneland also becomes the first racetrack in the United States

Former and current jockeys at a signing event

to offer Trakus video race technology. Trakus provides the ability — via sensor chips carried in saddlecloths and antennae positioned around the racetrack — to track each horse in a race electronically and digitally in real time. Information on individual horses is collected and displayed in various viewer-friendly animated forms … Keeneland's fall meeting, the first to be conducted over the new Polytrack surface, proves popular with patrons and horsemen alike, producing record handle and attendance and average field size of 10.02 starters per race. Fans wager a fall meet record total of $140,408,982. Keeneland also sets a single-day fall meet handle record of $12,733,860 and a single-day fall meet attendance record of 28,880 on opening Saturday. Total wagering during the fall meet averages a record $8,259,352 per day, while on-track attendance totals a record 233,218 … Keeneland also enjoys a record-setting sales year. The September yearling sale — the highest-grossing Thoroughbred auction in the world — realizes records for gross sales ($399,791,800), average ($112,427), and median ($108,420) and number of horses sold (3,556). Thirty-two yearlings sell for $1 million or more, including a colt by Kingmambo that brought a final bid of $11.7 million, the second-highest price for a yearling sold at public auction, from John Ferguson on behalf of Sheikh Mohammed bin Rashid al Maktoum. The November breeding stock sale grosses a near-record $313,843,800 and is highlighted by the sale record prices of $6.1 million for a horse in training, $2.4 million for a weanling filly, and a North American record price of $2.7 million for a weanling colt sold at public auction.

2007

A Mineshaft filly that worked an eighth of a mile in :9.3, a world-record equaling time for a juvenile auction work at that distance, brings a record bid of $1.75 million from B. Wayne Hughes at the April two-year-olds in training sale. It is the highest price ever paid for a filly at the April sale … The first spring race meeting conducted over Polytrack generates records for total wagering ($158,368,308), average daily wagering ($10,557,887), interstate commingled wagering ($125,952,284), and average daily interstate handle ($8,396,819). A single-day attendance record of 33,821 is set on Saturday, April 21. Keeneland sets wagering records for all sources handle as well as Pick Six, Pick Four, and Pick Three pools on Toyota Blue Grass Day. Total wagering on the ten-race Blue Grass card is a record $19,246,840, eclipsing the $18,319,492 wagered on the 2006 Blue Grass Day card … Keeneland's seventeen-day fall meet establishes attendance and wagering records. FallStars Weekend is expanded to include nine stakes — four of which are grade I events — worth $3.35 million. FallStars Saturday sets a single-day fall meet wagering record of $14,135,204. Total on-track attendance of 239,296 betters the previous fall's record and ranks as the second-largest attendance in track history. A fall meet Friday record crowd of 20,024 is set on College Scholarship Day … Keeneland auctions generate total sales of more than $815 million in 2007, driven by record gross figures for the January horses of all ages sale ($72,868,200), near-record levels for the September yearling sale ($385,018,600), and record November breeding stock sale ($340,877,200). Thirty-nine horses sell for $1 million or more at the November sale, equaling the record total sold in November 2000. Among them is Playful Act, a group I stakes-winning mare by Sadler's Wells, bringing a world-record $10.5 million from John Ferguson, on behalf of Sheikh Mohammed bin Rashid al Maktoum. The mare is part of the dispersal of the late Robert Sangster's Swettenham Stud.

2008

Keeneland reports the second-highest attendance and wagering figures in spring meet history — 243,606 and $150.5 million, respectively — for its sixteen-day spring meeting. Wagering records are set in the Toyota Blue Grass, with a twelve-horse field, the largest since 1983 … Keeneland realizes it's fourth-highest grossing September yearling sale ever, with sales totaling nearly $328 million, despite a global economic crisis. Eighteen yearlings sell for $1 million or more, including the sale-topping A.P. Indy filly out of Chimichurri that brought a final bid of $3.1 million from John Ferguson, on behalf of Sheikh Mohammed bin

Rashid al Maktoum … Keeneland records near-record attendance of 239,117 for its 2008 fall race meeting, the second-largest fall meet attendance in Keeneland history. A fall meet Friday record crowd of 22,052 is set on College Scholarship Day. During the fall meet Keeneland becomes the first racetrack in North America to provide live race coverage and limited simulcasts in high-definition format … Alma Haggin, credited with creating Keeneland's distinctive ambiance, dies in January at the age of ninety-five. Mrs. Haggin was the daughter of Keeneland co-founder and inaugural president Hal Price Headley; wife of Louis Lee Haggin II, who succeeded his father-in-law as president and later served as chairman of the board; and mother of Keeneland director and trustee Louis Lee Haggin III. William T. "Buddy" Bishop III, whose lifelong service to Keeneland included positions as director, secretary, trustee, and counsel, dies in April.

Michael Tabor becomes the 15th recipient of the coveted gold tray. Preceding him are Juddmonte Farms (fall 2005), Sam-Son Farm (spring 2005), Overbrook Farm (spring 2001), William Farish (fall 1993), Allen Paulson (spring 1993), Darby Dan Farm (fall 1988), Mr. and Mrs. Bertram Firestone (fall 1981), C.V. Whitney (fall 1976), Golden Chance Farm (fall 1976), Bwamazon Farm (fall 1972), T.A. Grissom (spring 1969), J. Graham Brown (spring 1965), Claiborne Farm (spring 1957) ,and Hasty House Farm (spring 1955).

2009

The Horseplayers Association of North America ranks Keeneland first among 65 of the continent's top racetracks in its inaugural Track Rating System. … A crowd of 33,680 — the second largest in Keeneland history — turns out Saturday, April 18, for Coolmore Lexington Stakes Day. Riders Up!, a karaoke competition at the Keeneland Entertainment Center, attracts a capacity crowd of 500 people and raises more than $50,000 for the Permanently Disabled Jockeys Fund. Keeneland concludes its spring race meeting with total attendance of 240,755, the third highest in track history, and an increase in average daily on-track wagering … Four yearlings bring $1 million or more at the September yearling sale, led by Storm 'n Indian, purchased for $2.05 million by John Ferguson for Sheikh Mohammed bin Rashid al Maktoum. From the last

Peb illustration of Ted Bassett, Queen Elizabeth II, Keith Allen, Will Farish, Bill Greely, and Jim Williams

full crop of leading sire Storm Cat, the colt is the first foal of champion mare Fleet Indian … Keeneland simulcasts its racing product in high definition beginning with the fall meet. Mr. and Mrs. William Shively's Dixiana Farm is named the new sponsor for the grade I Breeders' Futurity. Total wagering increases 8.7 percent during the 17-day fall meet … The November breeding stock sale is boosted by the near-record dispersal of the W.T. Young family's Overbrook Farm. With Eaton Sales as agent, Overbrook sells 148 horses for $31,760,000. When combined with the 48 yearlings Overbrook sold for $6,644,000 in September, the dispersal ranks as the second largest in Keeneland sales history, selling a total of 196 horses for $38,404,000, for an average of $195,939. Only the Nelson Bunker Hunt dispersal, which sold 580 horses for $46,912,800 during the 1988 January Horses of All Ages Sale, ranks higher … Pierre Bellocq, the internationally celebrated artist better known as "Peb," joins Keeneland and Daily Racing Form to announce the donation of nearly a half-century of his humorous caricatures and equine cartoons to the Keeneland Library … Jim Williams, Keeneland's longtime director of communications, retires following more than 38 years with the company … Central Bank becomes the signature sponsor of the 2010 Ashland Stakes … Keeneland is named winner of the 2009 Simulcast Award at the 17th annual International Simulcasting Conference in Saratoga Springs, New York. Keeneland also won the award, which honors the horse racing industry's best simulcast production, in 2003 and 2008.

2010

For the second consecutive year, the Horseplayers Association of North America (HANA) ranks Keeneland first among 69 of the continent's top racetracks in its Track Rating System...

In response to the changing needs of its consignors and buyers, Keeneland officials announce a new format for the 2010 September Yearling Sale. Highlights of the new format, developed by Keeneland in collaboration with its customers, include: a Book 1 select sale of 200 yearlings on opening Sunday night and Monday night; a vibrant, comprehensive Book 2 sale of 1,300 yearlings (roughly 325 horses per day in alphabetical order) from Tuesday through Friday; then following a "dark" day on Saturday, Keeneland will continue to offer a diverse selection of yearlings for a growing buying bench, both domestically and internationally... Keeneland's 2010 spring race meet establishes two attendance records. The track hosts a record opening-day crowd of 24,734, shattering the previous mark of 21,371 set in the spring of 1978. On Saturday, April 10, a record crowd of 33,727 turn out to watch Stately Victor make history by becoming the longest shot to win the $750,000 Toyota Blue Grass (G1).

A RACETRACK FOR THE PEOPLE

SHARON M. REYNOLDS

Keeneland was conceived by Bluegrass horsemen who wanted a track nearby to test their Thoroughbreds. But the savvy founders realized they needed to enlist the support of the community to establish their dream racetrack.

"We shall ask the good will and the active cooperation of many," they stated in their proposal, "for this is an enterprise which, if it proves successful, will be an everlasting credit to the sport of racing, not only in Kentucky, but throughout America."

The self-appointed committee of sportsmen who initiated the idea for Keeneland then turned the project over to a newly elected committee of ten native Kentuckians. The committee was charged with "testing the sentiment of the people of Lexington and the Bluegrass" for a racetrack that would operate "upon a no-profit and sportsmanlike basis."

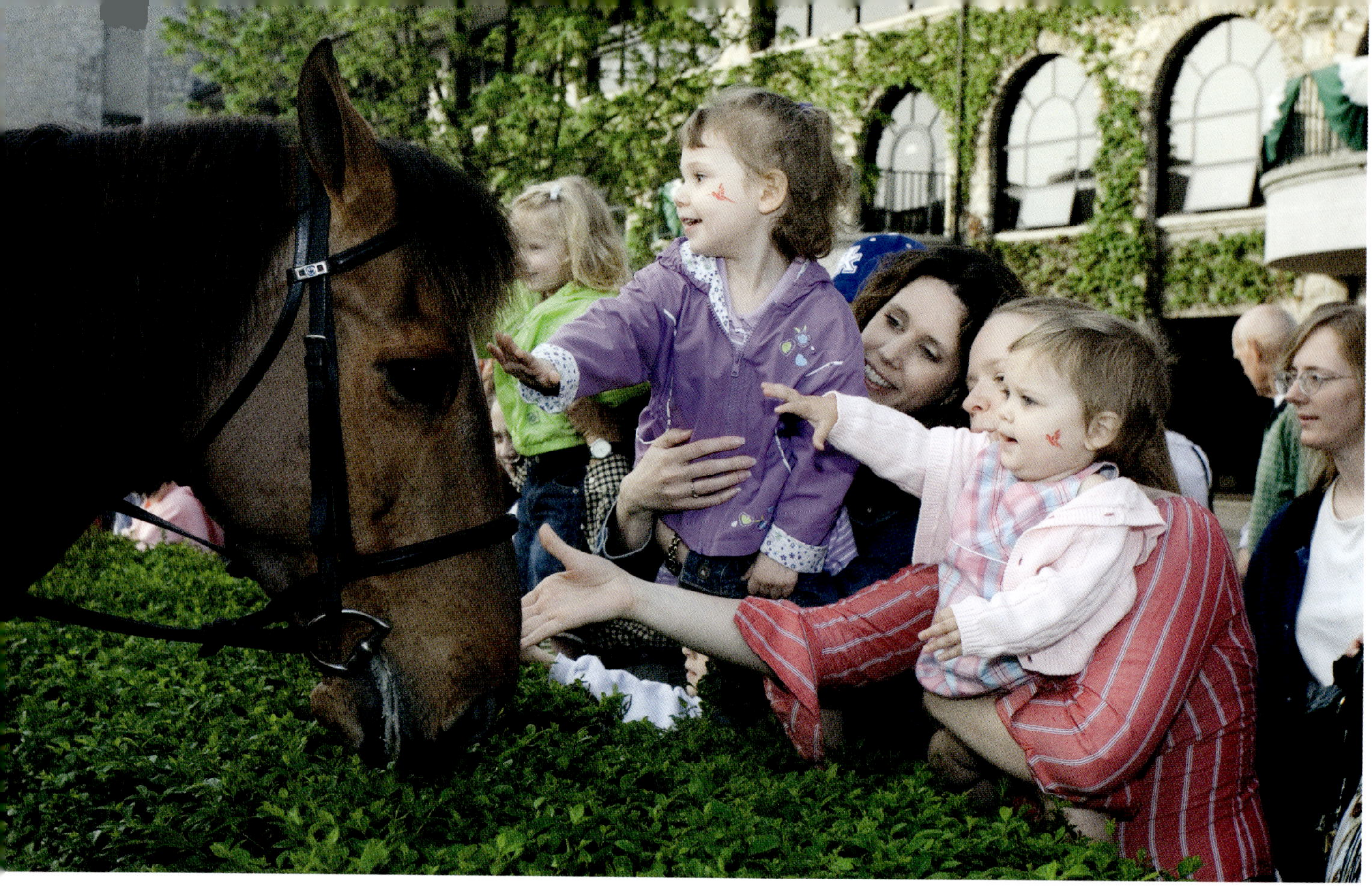

Keeneland's founders sought the "goodwill of many" in their proposal to investors, promising the track would be an "everlasting credit to the sport of racing."

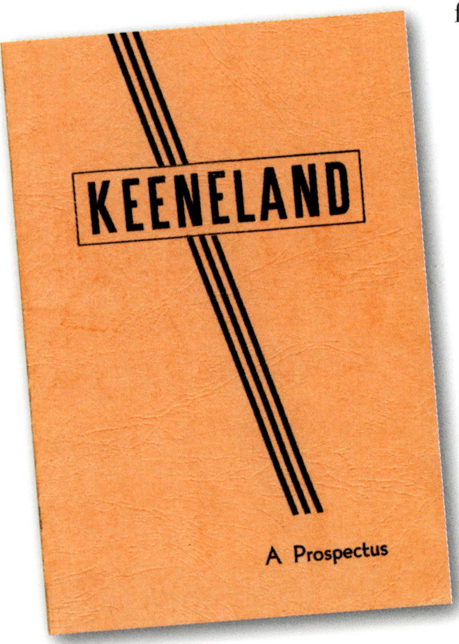

The founders' intent to organize the racecourse as a nonprofit entity met with skepticism in many quarters. There were plenty of naysayers in the Thoroughbred industry as well as the business community. John Clark, in his book *Trader Clark*, quotes some of the reaction.

"Keeneland will never make it," one critic declared. "It's way out in the country with no public transportation … no free passes … no public address system … gets its water from Manchester spring, which it sure as hell will pump dry."

But on opening day in October 1936, 8,000 people flocked to what was touted as "a model race track." During the nine-day meet, half the population of Lexington would come out to see the races.

The ties between town and track became even stronger over the years. As a testimony to this relationship, when Saint Joseph Hospital, then Lexington's only city hospital, opened its present quarters on Harrodsburg Road on June 19, 1959, Keeneland closed for two days so its employees, using Keeneland trucks, could help with the move.

CHARITY BEGINS AT HOME

Philanthropy helped cement Keeneland's community connection in the early days and continues to do so today. On November 9, 1938, two years

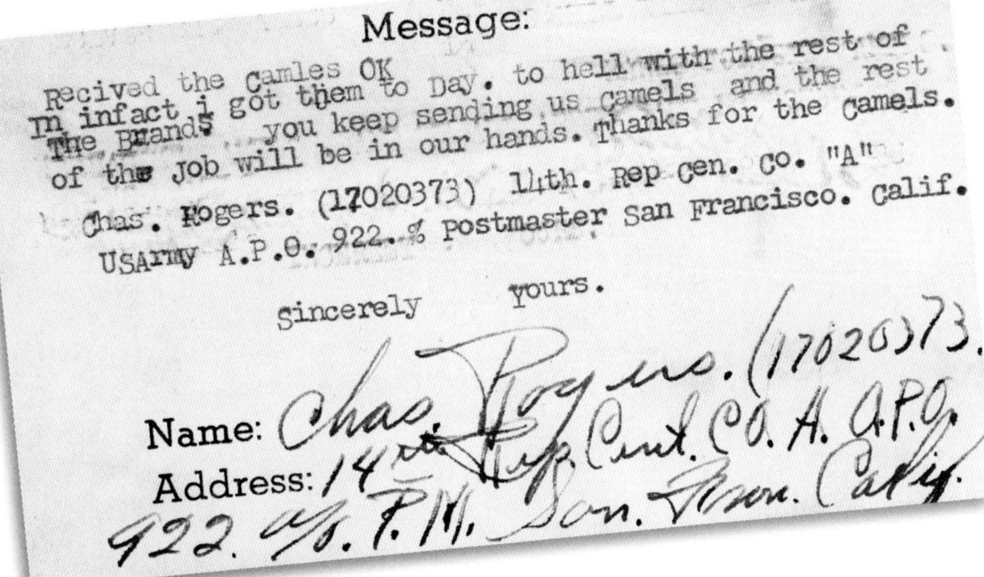

Keeneland's history of charitable giving included contributions to the Community War Chest during World War II; below, servicemen appreciated gifts such as cigarettes which the War Chest donations made possible.

after Keeneland was founded as the Keeneland Association, the race meetings showed a small profit and the association made its first charitable contribution — $500 to the Lexington Community Chest, a forerunner of United Way. That became the first of many donations to be awarded over the years.

During the 1940s the Keeneland Association was approved as a holding company, making it a tax-exempt organization. The war years brought an outpouring of gifts for the Lexington War Chest. One of the more widely appreciated gifts wasn't money but something not quite politically correct by twenty-first century standards — one million Camel cigarettes sent to U.S. servicemen overseas.

"Keep sending us Camels. To hell with the rest of the brands," wrote one GI, among the many who sent thank-you notes to Keeneland.

With the initiation of Thoroughbred auction sales in 1943, Keeneland had more revenue on hand to give. In 1944 the Keeneland Foundation was organized and incorporated as a nonprofit organization to make the best use of profits by establishing an endowment and distributing the funds to area charities. The foundation received an initial grant of $47,500 from the Keeneland Assocation, which remained the foundation's principal source of income.

CHARITABLE GIVING GROWS

During the 1950s Keeneland's philanthropic mission began to have a greater impact. A December 14, 1952, *Lexington Leader* article, headlined "Keeneland, Its Coffers Bulging Is Getting Ready to Play Santa Clause Again," proclaimed, "Charities and public-interest projects, which have received nearly $700,000 from the track since 1936, should get one of their biggest cuts yet. Keeneland reported a banner year of business."

Research, higher education, health, and general welfare were priorities for the Keeneland Foundation. Examples of early giving include the gift of an electron microscope in 1947 to the University of Kentucky, $200,000 in 1953 to build Keeneland Hall, a woman's dorm at UK; a commitment in the mid-1950s for $250,000 to the UK Agricultural Experiment station; $10,000 in 1954 to pay for the Salk vaccine for inoculating at-risk underprivileged children in the area; and in 1956, $15,600 in scholarships to seven Kentucky schools, including the University of Louisville, Eastern Kentucky University, Western Kentucky University, Morehead College, and Murray State.

Through the years, Keeneland has welcomed members of the military, treating them with respect and gratitude.

In 1960 a change in tax laws would drastically impact Keeneland's contributions program. Keeneland was forced to drop its nonprofit status and the decision was made to dissolve the foundation. Charitable giving went from an average of $100,000 a year in the five preceding years to $12,000 the first year after the law changed. Keeneland Foundation would be officially resurrected April 24, 2000, as a nonprofit organization. The 501 (c) 3 status now allows Keeneland to accept contributions and give donors a tax exemption for their gifts.

But in the days after the foundation closed philanthropy suffered. In the late 1960s and 1970s, charitable giving began creeping back to the level of the late 1950s. And in 1978 and 1979, Keeneland was handing out sums of more than $100,000 a year. From there, it took off.

At the height of the Thoroughbred sales boom in the mid-1980s, Keeneland donated more than $300,000 a year and in 1985 gave the largest donation to-date — $1 million to the University of Kentucky for the Maxwell A. Gluck Equine Research Center.

A $1 million gift from Keeneland helped start the Maxwell A. Gluck Equine Research Center.

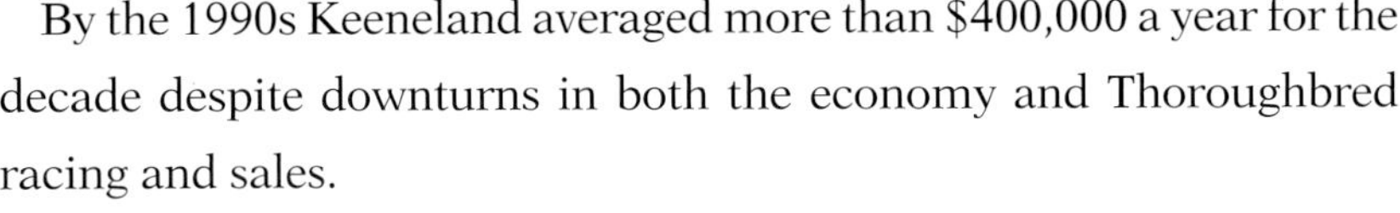

By the 1990s Keeneland averaged more than $400,000 a year for the decade despite downturns in both the economy and Thoroughbred racing and sales.

Keeneland's giving reached new heights in the twenty-first century with three consecutive years of annual charitable giving surpassing the $1 million mark. Another aspect of Keeneland's charitable giving program is advocacy. Keeneland partners are a myriad of nonprofit agencies in the region that make the community a better place to live and work. They range from the YMCA of Central Kentucky and the Bluegrass Animal Welfare League to the Bluegrass Conservancy and the Carnegie Center for Literacy and Learning.

MORE THAN RACES

Over the years Keeneland has become a popular place not just for racing but for community events, picnics, reunions, and outings. In 1938 and 1939, for example, the Thoroughbred Club of America held yearling judging contests on the grounds of Keeneland, with club members and the general public choosing the best colts and fillies.

Lexington Leader turf writer Jobie Arnold, in a May 13, 1965, column about renovations at Keeneland, noted that, " … Keeneland is open to the public, with many churches and organizations using the spacious grounds for picnics, concerts and friendly gatherings."

An October 12, 1969, photo spread in the *Lexington Herald-Leader* proclaimed, "During the 'Off-season' months of May, June, July and August, 100 civic, business, political, religious, fraternal, labor, youth, educational, agricultural and other organizations have used the Keeneland facilities … free of charge …"

Some of the typical yearly activities pictured in the article included the Aberdeen-Angus Futurity, Kennel Club Show, Governors' Conference, Antique Car Show, and Rotary Club outing for handicapped children.

The Keeneland Pony Club, which now meets at Masterson Station Park, got its start in 1958 at Keeneland Race Course. Members trained and competed there, and at one time the national championship rally was held at Keeneland.

Founders were John W. Greathouse Sr., Katherine Martin West, Mildred Martin Buster, and Stoney Johnson.

CELEBRATING 75 YEARS OF TRADITION

Keeneland's purchase and renovation of Keene Place has afforded another venue for community events; below, the Maker's Mark bottle signing always draws a big crowd; bottom, Keeneland president Nick Nicholson and Kentucky First Lady Jane Beshear wear pink to promote breast cancer research.

The pony club has become a tradition for many families. Greathouse's children John Jr., Nancy, and Allen were members, and Allen's children Nicholas and Michael are current members. Likewise, Susan Abner and Dorothy Curlin's children are among several others following in a parent's footsteps. Other notable past members include well-known horse trainer John Ward; the late Keeneland trustee William T. "Buddy" Bishop, son of Keeneland's first general manager; and Airdrie Stud manager Tim Thornton.

The demand on Keeneland for these events escalated during the 1960s and early 1970s as the association struggled to handle them. No other such community facility existed until the Kentucky Horse Park opened its gates in 1978. The park immediately became the new home for many of the events previously held at Keeneland and helped populate the park's calendar of events from the first year forward.

KEENELAND AND THE DERBY

The legendary Lexington Ball, once a premier social event held on the eve of Keeneland's Blue

Each fall Keeneland hosts Military Day to honor members of the Armed Services.

Grass Stakes, made its debut at Keeneland in April 1970. Pouring rains soaking the racetrack that day also flooded the floor of the big white tent that was all ready set up for dinner and dancing. Key organizers Juliette Trapp, Helen Mayes, Jessica Bell, and Carey Ellis recruited an army of volunteers to move tables onto a protected area beneath the clubhouse.

"It was a grand and glorious time, probably the best one we ever had," Bell said in an article about the ball appearing in *Keeneland* magazine.

The Lexington Ball is still an elegant affair, although it is now held on the eve of the Kentucky Derby and usually at Thoroughbred farms such as Spendthrift and Donamire Farm.

In recent years Keeneland has become one of the liveliest places to be, short of Churchill Downs, on Derby Day. The tradition of Derby parties found its ultimate expression at what is billed unofficially as "the world's largest Derby Party." Each year, throngs of up to 25,000 have gathered on the grounds, watching TVs in the paddock, poring over racing forms, and picnicking. Many arrive as early as 5:30 a.m. to contend for prime viewing spots.

With the growing number of large public events, requiring that huge tents be set up, it soon became obvious that Keeneland needed more space. In the late 1990s the

10,000-square-foot Entertainment Center was built, adjoining the Keene Barn and located next to the library. It's ideal for large meetings and receptions and can accommodate up to 500 guests. It's become a popular venue for weddings, and there have even been a few funerals and visitations held at the barn. Although Keeneland doesn't encourage it, some long-time fans of racing have quietly had their ashes spread on the property.

Nick Nicholson, Keeneland president, worked hard to acquire another public locale — the old Keene place, which had stood empty and largely unnoticed on the grounds of Keeneland for years. Once the home of John Keene, it has been given a new life, completely renovated, and is available to the public. Standing on fourteen acres in the midst of Keeneland Race Course property, it is the only place in Lexington where the Marquis de Lafayette, for whom Fayette County is named, ever slept. Keene Place can be rented to the public for meetings, community and charity events, restoration seminars, pre-horse-sale brunches, after-race cocktail parties, and wedding receptions.

The Budweiser Clydesdales are always a popular attraction at the track; Jim Williams, former director of communications for Keeneland, "interviews" a future racing fan at Breakfast with the Works.

COMBINING GIVING WITH COMMUNITY ACTIVITIES

Much of Keeneland's philanthropy involves both financial and in-kind sponsorships for many popular community events held on the grounds.

BLUE GRASS TRUST ANTIQUE & GARDEN SHOW

With Keeneland's strong ties to history, it's the perfect setting for the Bluegrass Trust for Historic Preservation's major fundraiser, the annual antiques and garden show. The show, which was previously held at Heritage Hall in downtown Lexington, moved to the Keene Barn and Entertainment Center in 1998. It's proven to be an excellent means of connecting Keeneland with non-racing audiences, drawing some 5,000 shoppers from across the region and the Midwest. Meanwhile, the sixty exhibitor spots at the show are quickly snapped up by antiques vendors and more vendors are on the waiting list. Garden exhibitors have a 7,000-square-foot tent to showcase their talents and displays, making the garden portion of the show an attraction in and of itself. The show has received attention from tourism groups and been featured in *Architectural Digest*. The Southeast Tourism Society named the show one of the region's top twenty events of 2003, and the Kentucky Tourism Council also honored it as a top ten festival or event for 2004.

Many activities for children make Breakfast with the Works a popular family event. Former jockey Patti Cooksey demonstrates the Equicizer with a young fan.

TASTE OF THE BLUEGRASS

Taste of the Bluegrass, an annual fundraiser for God's Pantry Food Bank, is held in the Keene Barn & Entertainment Center and showcases the very best food and drink Central Kentucky has to offer. The event features more than sixty food and beverage purveyors, live music, and a silent auction with a goal of raising money to defeat hunger in Kentucky.

KEENELAND CONCOURS D'ELEGANCE

The Southeast Tourism Society has judged this crowd-pleasing event one of the top twenty in the region for three consecutive years. The four-day affair has drawn automobile aficionados from all over the country to Keeneland since 2004. The concours features antique, vintage, rare, and prototype and concept autos. One particular model is celebrated each year, such as the iconic British Morgan, the Corvette, or the Ferrari. Proceeds from the concours go to the Kentucky Children's Hospital and to WUKY.FM radio.

Keeneland Concours
d'Elegance draws
car enthusiasts from
around the country.

EVERYBODY'S KEENELAND

In the mid-1990s Keeneland faced the challenge of a dwindling customer base. Many of the older race fans associated with the Thoroughbred industry were literally dying out, and Keeneland, with its focus on racing and sales, had come to be viewed as something of an ivory tower. At the same time, many events previously held at Keeneland had moved to the Kentucky Horse Park, which was better equipped to handle them.

In order to bring young people and families back to a racetrack once touted as "for the people," Keeneland charted a new course. The position of market development administrator was created in 1996 and a renewed emphasis placed on rebuilding the bridge to the community with efforts such as these:

Keeneland's popular Breakfast with the Works event, held each Saturday morning during the race meetings, was revamped. When free children's activities, a media sponsor (WLEX-TV), and a more elaborate subsidized buffet breakfast were added, attendance skyrocketed.

Over the past decade and a half, the number of eighteen- to twenty-four-year-olds coming to the track has more than doubled. College Scholarship Day at the spring and fall meets has been hugely successful. Students vie for ten $1,000 scholarships given away by Keeneland and are given free passes to return to the track later in the meet.

More special events were added to expand Keeneland's sponsorship program — not only to underwrite the racing purse structure, but also to bring in new fans. One of the most successful partnerships has been with Makers Mark, which produces special edition bottles released on opening day of the spring meet. This partnership has simultaneously helped boost the Keeneland fan base and generated millions of dollars for charitable programs through sales of the bottles.

For Keeneland's seventieth anniversary, original art was commissioned for the Keeneland Gift Shop — one series very contemporary, the other, stylized folk art. Those pieces, in addition to the traditional racing art found in the Keeneland shop, appeal to a wide range of tastes — a Keeneland for everyone.

The founders of Keeneland would no doubt approve of these marketing efforts. "Keeneland was established for three purposes," says Louis Haggin III, son of long-time Keeneland president Louis Haggin II, "for the horse, the owner and the community. That hasn't changed over the years."

KEENELAND
LIBRARY

Erich L. Ruehs

The precise date of the world's first library is uncertain. In ancient Mesopotamia, scholars could access information, but clay tablets, not books, were the medium some 5,000 years ago. Paper wouldn't come along for another three millennia, give or take. But in 1939, when Keeneland Association director W. Arnold Hanger donated 2,300 rare books pertaining solely to the topic of Thoroughbreds, what resulted was a repository whose collection leaves little room for ambiguity. Today, the world's finest collection of Thoroughbred erudition consists of over 10,000 volumes of books, 1,500 videocassettes, a quarter million photos and photographic negatives, and tens of thousands of periodicals. And then there are the collections donated by the *Daily Racing Form*. This significant compilation, dating back to 1896, is estimated to be in the neighborhood of 11 million total pages.

Laura Hillenbrand, author of *Seabiscuit: An American Legend*, has a particular appreciation for the library's content. "In this building," said Hillenbrand, "in the Keeneland Library, the past lives alongside the present. It was in the volumes in this place that I *found* Seabiscuit, dead a generation before I was born, yet living and breathing in all his immediacy, as real as the twin spires at Churchill."

Published in 2001, the book was a hit, winning the William Hill Sports Book of the Year award. Two years later, *Seabiscuit* hit the big screen and was nominated for seven Academy Awards. The film, starring Jeff Bridges and Tobey Maguire, would take in a worldwide gross of almost $130 million. "The beauty of the Keeneland Library is that in its magnificent archives, all of racing's greats are immortal, living forever in the supreme moments of their youth," stated Hillenbrand. "Racing is a sport of many treasures. None greater than this one."

 But it was six decades before Hillenbrand's unearthing of Seabiscuit when Keeneland Library debuted in the fall of 1940. The original library was located on the second floor of Keeneland's clubhouse, directly above what is today the south grandstand entrance. At first, the library would average less than one information seeker a day, and often a week would pass without a single patron entering the library. And that's how it would remain for some time. However, this was hardly viewed as a dilemma. Keeneland Library was not the result of popular demand, nor was it built with the intentions of becoming a "commercial success." Something much deeper was taking place.

Although Keeneland's original prospectus, created in 1935, makes no mention of a library, it does maintain that Keeneland's creation was to be a paradigm for Thoroughbred racing and perpetuate the sport based on its finest traditions. Keeneland president Nick Nicholson is a disciple of this philosophy. "From the very beginning, this library was a clear, irrefutable indication that this new racetrack was going to be something different," he stated. "Here was an institution that was going to perform a substantive service to the business of Thoroughbred racing, and even in our infancy, wanted to improve every aspect of this esteemed industry."

Hanger's initial gift of 2,300 volumes represented a truly remarkable anthology. The collection was originally assembled by a New York lawyer and bibliophile, Robert Turnbull, who spent twenty-seven years amassing his own Turf library. Turnbull traveled

Left, a few of the more than 10,000 books housed in the library; below, Keeneland general manager William T. Bishop, standing, and Amelia Buckley host a meeting in the library.

throughout France, England, and the United States where he attended auctions, sought out booksellers, and solicited private owners for their very best wares. Turnbull then read and personally assessed every volume. Many books were discarded regardless of their monetary worth as it was academic value being sought. Earnest R. Gee, who ran the nation's largest agency dealing in the field of Thoroughbred literature and art, brokered the deal between Hanger and Turnbull. The January 6, 1940, issue of *The Blood-Horse* called the Turnbull collection "America's most comprehensive collection of books on Thoroughbred breeding and

racing." But Hanger's contribution would not stand alone on the shelves for long.

Benefactors such as Hal Price Headley (Keeneland's first president), Robert Livingston Gerry Sr., and Pierre Lorillard soon made contributions from their private libraries. In 1954 Hanger would follow his literary gift with the entire C.C. Cook photographic negative collection consisting of 20,000 glass and film negatives taken by one of America's first professional Thoroughbred photographers. The C.C. Cook collection includes virtually every major figure involved in the Sport of Kings from 1900 to 1952. In 1961 Hanger and Headley secured the Bernard Stanley Morgan collection of negatives. Louis Lee Haggin II (Keeneland president 1956-70) was also instrumental in bringing Morgan's staggering collection of 150,000 black and white negatives to the library. Spanning more than a quarter century (1935-1961), Morgan's images, like C.C. Cook's, feature anybody that was somebody in racing at the time. Also part of the library's photographic collection are "Skeets" Meadors' negatives from 1947-67, which include some 5,000 items, and the work of John C. Hemment, whose 3,500 photos cover almost every major Thoroughbred

Other historic photos include one of the 1895 Suburban Handicap run at old Coney Island racetrack and Colonel E.R. Bradley, inset, center.

event that took placc in New York from 1890 through 1910.

The number of books would steadily increase as well, and by the mid-seventies space was becoming a serious concern. By 1986 the library underwent a major expansion, doubling in size to more than 3,000 square feet. Three years later a storage area was created on the third floor of the clubhouse in an attempt to contain an ever-evolving collection of any and all items pertaining to the Thoroughbred. But the expanding collection would push the limits of even this enlarged space. In 1997, Marylou Whitney, whose philanthropy is legendary, contributed more than 1,000 highly regarded texts from the Whitney family library. The Keeneland Library's collection now numbered well over 7,000 books. And then the *Daily Racing Form* would enter the picture in 2000 by donating its entire archives including the *Morning Telegraph* and the *American Racing Manual*. This contribution would have to arrive by way of two eighteen-wheeler tractor-trailers. At this point a new location was no longer a luxury, but a necessity, if Keeneland's preservation mission was to evolve into the new millennium.

Ground was broken in the spring of 2001 on the site of what would become the new library. This building would stand on a hill adjacent to the Keene Barn and Entertainment Center, seven-tenths of a mile east of its previous location.

First-time visitors may be excused for initially mistaking this outstanding structure for anything but a library. After all, most libraries don't consist of 325 tons of hand-chiseled Kentucky limestone. Architect Morio Kow was as dramatic as he was restrained in diagramming a building that seamlessly blends into an already dazzling landscape. "You'll never know it wasn't always there," reflected Kow, whose design thrives with all the amenities of a twenty-first-century complex while proudly standing as a gallant edifice whose architectural derivation is pure Kentucky. Only an interesting challenge would arise before the first stone was put into place. The Keene Barn, along with the surrounding buildings, all feature limestone that was cut using early twentieth-

From left to right, trustee Louis L. Haggin, president Nick Nicholson, librarian Cathy Schenck, chairman emeritus James E. Bassett, and trustee Charles Nuckols cut the ribbon for the new library.

century technology. Moreover, the passage of time has resulted in a texture that can't be easily duplicated, particularly when factoring in light and shadows. This new building had to capture the sun in such a way that its veneer would emulate the appearance of the surrounding structures, particularly when viewed far afield.

John Howard has been the projects administrator for Keeneland since 1991 and best explains this achievement by walking right up to the new building and pointing out a single limestone block. "Look at how the shadow produced from this one stone is irregular. The last thing we wanted was a generic, institutional, straight-line look," he said. "When viewed from a distance, that would have completely changed the overall look." Success was attained only after each piece of limestone was individually sculpted, thus creating a structure not only worthy of its surroundings but its contents as well. "Even the dormers are constructed of this specially cut limestone," says Howard. "Drive around and tell me how often you see stone dormers, even in Kentucky." But as gorgeous as this building is

Morio Kow designed the library to appear as if it has always been part of the Keeneland landscape.

from the outside, it's what lies within that makes the library the intellectual mecca for Thoroughbred devotees.

Inside a cathedral ceiling soars above flanking trophy cases whose awards, and other riches, seemingly echo with the thunder of a champion's gallop. Three massive arched windows on both ends of the main room are as elegant as they are functional, as the northeast end of the building finds the morning sun while the southwest captures the afternoon. Additional light comes courtesy of eight dormers and a cupola with four windows. And then there are the eleven colossal ceiling lights whose 1920s reproduction design seamlessly interacts with the contemporary environment. The interior was designed by William Hodgins Inc. from Boston. The firm's namesake was specific when creating an environment that would appeal to both genders. "We wanted surroundings that men, too, would find appealing so we went with natural colors and strived for an atmosphere that was comfortable yet energizing, but most of all natural," said Hodgins.

Visitors have ten reading tables and thirty-six chairs from which to choose. The furniture was custom made and designed to hide wires, thus preserving a non-technological feel despite compatibility with all modern devices. Each of the ten black walnut tables can accommodate laptops. For a more tucked away feeling there are also twelve cubicles, three of which are equipped with Internet-ready computers. The remaining nine cubicles serve as private work areas and microfilm stations, and can even come equipped with a TV and VCR for reviewing past races. For formal or informal meetings there are two conference rooms that can each comfortably fit ten to twelve people. These rooms may be used by members of the

A cathedral ceiling is one of the library's signature features as is museum-quality artwork, below, bronzes are part of the art collection housed in the Keeneland Library.

Thoroughbred community or serious researchers free of charge. Each conference room is wired for laptops and has retractable screens for PowerPoint presentations. Both also feature an adjoining patio ideal for a breath of fresh air or a cell phone call.

Even for a 10,000-square-foot structure, there's a remarkable use of space. What's just

Natural colors and rich woodwork create an inviting ambience; below, an antique jockey scale

as notable is how the new library (almost seven times the size of its predecessor in 1940) has managed to retain the cozy ambiance of a living room or parlor.

But no library, regardless of content and décor, is complete without an accomplished staff. James E. "Ted" Bassett III, who is undisputedly credited by his peers as one of the most important individuals behind Keeneland's success, proudly affirms: "The hallmark of the Keeneland Library is its total commitment to those in search of historical information of the Thoroughbred." Keeneland's retired chairman of the board and current trustee emeritus is quick to credit the people who have maintained the library over the years. "Indeed, Keeneland Library's distinguishing characteristic is the loyal dedication of its librarians, from Amelia Buckley to Cathy Schenck and her associate Phyllis Rogers, who have responded to inquiries from all corners of the world," he said. Bassett also references his late friend, Joe Hirsch, the acclaimed turf columnist for the *Daily Racing Form* and founder of the National Turf Writers Association. "I can't tell you how many times I'd hear Joe say: 'Whenever in doubt of sire or dam, or who or where, or win or lose, call the Keeneland Library.'"

As a research library, Keeneland offers comfortable areas to review materials such as the fragile early text, below.

"This library has something for everyone," says Cathy Schenck, who began working at Keeneland Library in April 1978. "There is fiction, poetry, history, biographies, equine art, along with books on feeding, breeding theories, training, handicapping, pedigrees, race records, and more."

And the most frequently asked question? "I would have to say biographical questions about individual jockeys or trainers, including their career statistics. Race records or a specific chart for a particular horse are common, too."

But queries are by no means restricted, and there are no parameters for the curious. "We receive over 4,000 visitors a year along with thousands of phone calls and e-mails," acknowledged the head librarian, "and one thing I've learned is the questions can be as unique as the people asking them." The Smithsonian, network television, *Sports Illustrated*, and ESPN have all employed the library's invaluable resources as have museums spanning North America. But the individual in pursuit of his or her own form of enlightenment is just as welcome.

Sorting through the tens of millions of pages of text in any reference library can be a daunting task for the uninitiated whose mission is to locate even a single piece of information. But don't fret. Keeneland Library staff has the gift of making an arduous task seem almost routine. "Many people come in search of their ancestors," said Phyliss Rogers, who began working at Keeneland Library in early 1994. "We treat these genealogical searches with the utmost respect while at the same time not giving the researcher false hopes on what he or she may be able to find. So much can be lost in the vagaries of time." However, just as in handicapping, inevitable

This image from the Cook collection shows racing fans in front of the Hialeah tote board.

Photographs from the Hemment collection also are housed in the library as are rare editions of *Spirit of the Times.*

longshots are bound to defy the odds. One such example is the quest of Raymond Davis of Rockville, Maryland, who grew up hearing legendary tales about his mother's first cousin, "Uncle Art."

The mission Davis took on was nothing less than grand, as his intention was not only to seek genealogical enlightenment but to produce a self-published book chronicling his kin, who was the winning jockey in the 1908 Kentucky Derby. "Without the Keeneland Library and the services of the staff there would not have been a biography of Arthur Pickens," said Davis. "Their help in guiding me, a novice, in searching for a subject matter was immeasurable." Davis learned how to use the massive amounts of information literally at his fingertips. He soon found himself, thanks to some informal training by the librarians, in the role of researcher extraordinaire. "The tutorial acumen of the librarians in familiarizing me with the multiple resources of their library proved to be essential when it came to me locating and interpreting specific racing information on my cousin," acknowledged Davis. The resulting book, *Remembering Arthur Pickens*, reveals the many achievements of Davis' "Uncle Art," not the least of which was a victory in the 1908 Kentucky Derby aboard a 23-to-1 shot by the name of Stone Street. Davis reflects upon his book with a sense of sheer gratitude and appreciation. "I discovered the life profile of Arthur's career at the Keeneland Library. Almost each finding was euphoric."

Thoroughbred racing has always walked hand in hand with our

Sculptures by Jules Bonheurare are treasured pieces.

cultural history which, when viewed in a detailed manner, can be voluminous. This is best evidenced by standing in the library's humidity and temperature-controlled vault that holds almost every issue of the *Daily Racing Form* (dating back to 1896) and its sister publication, the *Morning Telegraph*. If stacked one-a-top the other, the total height of this collection would reach an estimated 560 feet, (the height of a forty-six-story building).

"Sitting within these piles of print is an irreplaceable part of our culture and the very history of our sport," said Nicholson. "Many of these newspapers of the time covered not only racing but the entertainment business as well. The history of the movies, early radio, and the formation of television is all here. Broadway plays, too."

But the sheer notion of randomly pouring through 11 million pages of text in search of a long-forgotten race might best be described as anesthetizing. That is, until the *Daily Racing Form* Preservation Project came along.

In 2007, the Keeneland Association and the University of Kentucky Libraries partnered

to preserve Keeneland's nearly complete collection of the *DRF* and the *Morning Telegraph*. Leading the pilot project was Becky Ryder, head of preservation services at the UK Libraries.

The preservation process involves separating the bound newspaper books into individual pages and carefully analyzing page order and physical condition. Some very fragile *DRF* issues, particularly those from the early 1900s and 1930s through the 1950s, require very careful handling.

After the physical preparation, a combination of microfilm and digital imaging is used to create an online archive. Software programs transform the images into searchable text. It is a massive, long-term project that will take years and millions of dollars to finish.

Upon its hopeful completion, the DRF Preservation Project will allow researchers to locate a precise piece of information in a matter of seconds. This search engine would be in the hands of anyone with a computer and an Internet connection, free of charge, thanks to a partnership between the Keeneland Association and the University of Kentucky.

"We've been fortunate enough to have been awarded a grant for the National Digital Newspaper Program with funding coming from the National Endowment for the Humanities," said Mary Molinaro, director of the Preservation and Digital Programs Department for the University of Kentucky. However, other sources of funding must be identified to ensure this historic endeavor is completed.

In addition to the wealth of printed material, Keeneland Library is a stellar museum in its own right. An original Thomas J. Coates painting became part of the library's collection in 2002 thanks to John and Luanne Milward of Lexington. Bronzes by acclaimed nineteenth-century French sculptor Isidore Jules Bonheur, whose work was commissioned for the Sultan of Constantinople's palace and England's King Edward VII, also are displayed in this building.

An absorbing exhibit is the Horseshoe Collection gifted from the family of Dr. Fred W. Rankin in 1954. "Dr. Rankin was an internationally known surgeon and one of the original founders of Keeneland Association," said Schenck. "Here's the actual shoe Man o' War wore in his last race on October 12, 1920, when he defeated Sir Barton."

Citation's 1948 Kentucky Derby shoe is there, along with a shoe worn by Longfellow, whose passing was national news. His November 7, 1893, obituary in the *New York Times* proclaimed him, "A magnificent animal both as a race horse and a sire." War Admiral and his nemesis, Seabiscuit, have shoes on display as well, and viewing them in person is indeed a moving experience. Nicholson often harkens back to W. Arnold Hanger when attempting to describe the library's essence: "Mr. Hanger once referred to the Keeneland Library as being the soul of Keeneland. He couldn't have been more right."

LIGHTS, CAMERA...
KEENELAND!

AVE LAWYER

Remember when the Kentucky Derby was run at Keeneland? How about the Breeders' Cup? Remember when Seabiscuit dueled with War Admiral in Lexington? When Secretariat outstripped the field in the Belmont as he crossed the finish line at Keeneland?

Magic moments all, but all fiction. All courtesy of the motion picture industry.

Many have experienced the magic that is Keeneland in person. Millions more worldwide have done so, courtesy of the film and television industry, top actors, directors, producers, and technicians. "What better opportunity," asked Keeneland president Nick Nicholson, "to showcase to a worldwide audience all that is beautiful about Keeneland, and to represent our industry in a positive light?"

A scene from *Seabiscuit* shows the "match race" between the star and War Admiral.

From top, celebrities at Keeneland have ranged from football great Gayle Sayers, Larry Hagman, and M.C. Hammer to, right, Priscalla Presley.

Keeneland's attraction for filmmakers is its quality of timeless elegance and tasteful simplicity. Time passes, things change, but within Keeneland's weathered walls the "feel" of the past endures. Production designers and set decorators love the fact that this twenty-first century racecourse can, with minimal dressing, pass for one almost 100 years in the past.

"Innovation! One cannot be forever innovating. I want to create classics," declared chic couturier, Coco Chanel. To the universal joy of filmmakers, those with their hands on the reins at Keeneland are as passionately committed to preserving what is classic, while thoughtfully embracing what is new.

"Hollywood thinks that this is special because it is special," said Nicholson to Lexington *Herald-Leader* writer Rich Copley. "What the movies do is have us look at Keeneland with fresh eyes, how Hollywood looks at it on the big screen."

Keeneland's movie career broke out of the gate in 1938 when scenes for a movie called *Kentucky*, a Romeo and Juliet story with a Bluegrass background, starring Loretta Young, Richard Green, and Walter Brennan, were shot in the Keeneland clubhouse.

THE THOROUGHBREDS / RUN FOR THE ROSES

Almost four decades later the Kentucky Derby sequence for a film called *The Thoroughbreds*, aka Run for the Roses, was filmed at the track.

Described by producer Mario Crespo, himself a Thoroughbred horse breeder at his Maple Lawn Farm, as the story of the ambition of every Thoroughbred owner to own a Kentucky Derby winner, the film starred Panchito Gomez, Vera Miles, and Stuart Whitman and was funded by local veterinarian Dr. Arnold G. Pessin and horseman Richard Rivers

Larry Dale Keeling, a staff reporter for the then Lexington *Herald*, recounted his experiences as an "atmosphere player" — an elevated term for an "extra" when, on a frosty day in October — a far cry from the first Saturday in May — cameras rolled on the scene in which an

Legendary sports broadcaster Howard Cosell interviews trainer Leroy Jolley in the Keeneland paddock.

embattled horse wins the Kentucky Derby. Keeling, with sixty or so other extras, "Froze myself solid for $5 a day and lunch, plus the opportunity to someday see myself — chill bumps and all — on the big screen."

Keeling recalls that for the most part, his "acting" consisted of cheering, for which he had a lot of practice during long afternoons at the track. But when his role was expanded to that of a successful bettor collecting his winnings, he commented wryly, "For that performance, I've had considerably less practice."

Bill Greely, track vice president at the time, entered into the spirit of the shoot by joining the cheering program-waving extras surrounding stars Vera Miles and Stuart Whitman. He recalled with amusement that what they cheered was not an actual race on the track but a white handkerchief on a stick, toted up and down the walkway by assistant director Murray Schwartz.

AND THEY'RE OFF

Quick! Name George Clooney's first movie.

Hats off if you said *And They're Off*. The film, starring Jose Ferrer (married at the time to George's aunt Rosemary), Miguel Ferrer, Tab Hunter, and Linda Purl, was partially shot at Keeneland during the spring meet in 1982.

George Clooney is quoted in an *Esquire* interview as saying, "I didn't even want to be an actor. I was just hanging out with my cousin (Miguel Ferrer). I rented my car, a Monte

Carlo, to (the movie crew) and got fifty bucks a day. They gave me a part as an extra. And Miguel said, 'Come to L.A. and be an actor.' I had just spent the summer cutting tobacco, which is a miserable job. So that's what made me move to Hollywood."

The film was never released, but Clooney's career was off and running.

BLUEGRASS

In 1987, several scenes for the made-for-TV movie *Bluegrass*, starring Cheryl Ladd, Wayne Rogers, Diane Ladd, and Mickey Rooney, were shot at Keeneland. Mickey Rooney's great friend Helen Hayes happened to be a guest of Mrs. A. B. Hancock at Claiborne Farm. When the two unexpectedly encountered each other in the Keeneland paddock after many years, they couldn't hide their joy.

Mickey Rooney and former Keeneland president Bill Greely share a laugh.

Robert Urich shoots a scene railside at Keeneland.

One Lexingtonian tells of handsome male friend who had signed on as a crowd scene extra. When it came time to shoot a close-up of Cheryl Ladd, director Simon Wincer was obviously unhappy with the scene. "Cut! Cut!" he yelled and scanned the crowd. Pointing at the tall, good-looking young man, he shouted, "You! Come stand right over here," indicating a spot directly in front of Ms. Ladd.

Thrilled and thinking his fifteen minutes of fame were upon him, the man needed no urging as he stepped to the spot across from the lovely Cheryl Ladd.

"Now turn around," barked the director.

"So I have my back to her?" asked the bewildered young man.

"Yes," said Wincer, obviously aggravated. "I need for you to block the sun!"

SARATOGA SUMMER/ A HORSE FOR DANNY

The next production to come calling was *Saratoga Summer*, (aka *A Horse For Danny*), a 1995 made-for-TV film starring Robert Urich and Leelee Sobieski. Sobieski played Danny Bara, an eleven-year-old who wins a dice throw for a small horse with incredible bloodlines, aptly named Tom Thumb.

Shooting was well underway when early one Sunday morning a ringing phone awakened Keeneland's governmental relations specialist, Judy Taylor, assigned to shepherd the production. It was a production manager desperately seeking a dentist for

From top, TV actor Tom Poston and family; actor and comedian Tim Conway in the paddock with jockey Pat Day and Keeneland's Jim Williams; teen heart-throb David Cassidy

Robert Urich who was stricken with toothache. Unfazed, Taylor tracked down her own dentist and prefaced her request that he come his office immediately to treat a new patient named Robert Urich with, "This is not a joke …"

After the appointment, she drove Urich, affable in spite of his pain, to the closest pharmacy, which happened to be in K-Mart on Nicholasville Road. She remembers being glad it was a Sunday morning so there weren't many people around. One kid did a double take on sighting the star, but shrugged and walked away, obviously thinking he'd made a mistake.

Taylor and Urich remained friends, exchanging Christmas cards until his untimely death in 2002.

During the production, Taylor claims to have "aged 100 years" when the dreaded words, "I smell smoke" rang out as the crew set up a shot in the sales pavilion,

"I said, stop, stop, stop! Everything stops until we find it. I was thinking, the sales pavilion is going to burn down on my watch and there's no place to hide where Mr. Bassett won't find me.

"We scoured every room, every cabinet, and every cupboard and found nothing.

"I was looking for a rocket ship to whisk me away to Mars when someone discovered a half-extinguished cigarette in a small garden patch under an air vent. The smell of the smoke was being sucked into the intake vent. I was never so relieved to see a cigarette butt in my life."

SEABISCUIT

Not many know that the 1938 Horse of the Year, Seabiscuit, who enjoyed much of his success in California, was actually foaled in Kentucky, at Claiborne Farm. Sixty-four years later, Seabiscuit came home to run what was called the biggest match race in history against War Admiral, the brilliant and temperamental offspring of Man o' War. But this time, the race was run not at Baltimore's Pimlico Race Course but at Keeneland.

Keeneland played a starring role in the movie *Seabiscuit*, including serving as the site for the historic match race.

Hollywood was back in the picture.

Seabiscuit, the film based on Laura Hillenbrand's best-selling book about the longshot that became a legend, was a joint production of Universal Pictures, DreamWorks Pictures, and Spyglass Entertainment, and starred Jeff Bridges, William H. Macy, Tobey Maguire, and Chris Cooper.

Because the real Pimlico was too modern for their purposes, producers Frank Marshall and Kathleen Kennedy set out in search of a track that looked true to the period and Keeneland fit the bill.

Crews toiled to transform the infield, track, grandstand, clubhouse, and lawn into Depression-era Pimlico. A winner's circle was installed on the clubhouse side of the grandstands. An observation tower loomed at the finish line, now sporting a period finish pole. Each box was emblazoned with a Pimlico insignia and wooden seats replaced modern metal ones. And, as it did on that first day in November 1938, the Maryland state flag whipped atop the new old-fashioned tote board in the infield.

Weeks before filming was to begin, a Keeneland staffer asked Nicholson what should be done with the boxes arriving in the mail. There were so many. All of uniform size and shape, all shipped from China, all addressed to Biggins Inc. c/o Keeneland.

The trickle became a spate and then a flood. The Keeneland dining room began to fill up with hundreds upon hundreds of boxes.

One day, there was a knock on Nicholson's door, and a young man stuck his head in and said, "Sir, my name is Joe Biggins. Might some boxes have arrived for me?"

The boxes, it turned out, contained the 7,210 inflatable dummies that were to be used, intermingled with live extras, to simulate the approximately 40,000 spectators who thronged the infield and grandstand at Pimlico for the race of the century. Movie history was about to be made at Keeneland.

Executive producer Steven Spielberg and writer and director Gary Ross were determined to make the racing sequences in Seabiscuit more exciting than any captured so far on film. Since the camera would now move along with the horses, the old cardboard cutouts, used to simulate crowds in the stands, were a no-go.

Joe Biggins, chief technician for the grandstand scene, pondered the problem. Surfing

Inflatable dummies dressed in vintage attire filled the Keeneland grandstand.

the net one night, he found a novelty plastics company in China that manufactured inflatable dummies. Could they ship a few prototypes right away? Certainly, they said, ship to whom? To Biggins Inc., improvised Biggins, and a startup company was created on the spot.

A delighted Gary Ross gave the idea the green light, and Biggins Inc. was off and running. The dummies were manufactured and shipped in record time. And in the Keeneland dining room, now transformed into an assembly line, the mountain of boxes continued to grow.

Working alone and against the clock, Biggins toiled, pump in hand, inflating dummy after dummy. When it became apparent the clock would win, Nicholson sent him to Two Keys, a popular local student hangout, to recruit reinforcements. With the help of five University of Kentucky students, the dummies were blown up, dressed in long-sleeved T-shirts with khaki or blue suits silk screened on them, and carefully set and tied down in the stands.

So well did they do their job that the raging storm that blew through Keeneland the night before the shoot barely disturbed their handiwork. All it did was jostle them enough that Kathleen Kennedy commented, "They're not all stick straight so they actually looked more like a real crowd."

"It's the Keeneland clubhouse, so they all have ties," Nicholson joked to *Herald-Leader* reporter Rich Copley.

This was the first time inflatable mannequins had been used to replicate a crowd in a movie. Pumped by this success, Biggins Inc. became The Inflatable Crowd Company Inc., which now has an impressive roster of film credits.

"I'll never forget Keeneland, because that's where I got my start," Nicholson quoted Biggins as saying. As for Nicholson, a souvenir dummy in his basement still inspires a smile.

As a cold November sun tinged the sky, more than 4,000 unpaid extras in their grandparents' clothes braved cold and cutting winds to be a part of the pivotal match race, Seabiscuit's centerpiece.

On War Admiral in the role of Charley Kurtsinger was Hall of Fame, two-time Kentucky Derby winner Chris McCarron. Now retired, McCarron was also the race designer for the film. Atop Seabiscuit was another Hall of Famer, champion jockey Gary Stevens in the role of George "The Iceman" Wolf.

Before the race, recalled Nicholson, McCarron started teasing Stevens that he wouldn't lay down on the match race. "I'm thinking about changing the script," he was heard to say. "It's a challenge," said McCarron to the Lexington *Herald-Leader's* Maryjean Wall, "to

Elisabeth Shue, Dakota Fanning, and Kurt Russell headlined the cast of *Dreamer*.

make it look like a jockey is down, riding hard, trying for everything when that jockey is supposed to lose the race." Not only that, but Thoroughbreds are naturally competitive. They're born to run and conditioned to win.

As the afternoon waned, it came time for the last shot: the epic homestretch battle between the two horses, in the last fifty yards of the 1 1/8 mile race. This being McCarron's only scene in the film, he wanted to look like he was really trying. Stevens, on the other hand, handed a win by history, was relaxed and confident.

The camera rolled and Gary Ross called "action!" In the actual race, Seabiscuit pulled ahead by a length, then two, then three, before winning by four. But in that first take on that frigid November afternoon sixty-four years later, history was rewritten by a horse who didn't know he'd been cast in the losing role.

McCarron tried his best not to look happy as War Admiral galloped across the finish line well ahead of Seabiscuit. Stevens was less pleased, and director Ross, aware of fast fading daylight and the urgency of getting this final climactic shot, was frantic.

Recalled Nicholson, "Gary yelled 'cut' and looked at me as if to say, "How did that happen?" And I told him, "Gary, you just learned how hard it is to fix a horse race. It's hard to tell the horses not to win!"

By the time the shot was re-set, a scant seven minutes of daylight remained. Ross assembled actors and crew and extras and impressed on them that the margin for error was absolutely zero.

The second time round, everything worked to perfection. Seabiscuit, in Red Pollard's immortal words, "made a Rear Admiral out of War Admiral." And crowd and jockey went wild.

"When you see the film," said Nicholson, "you think they're all celebrating Seabiscuit's victory. But the real story is Gary Ross is thrilled because they nailed the scene and got the shot. And the crowd swarming the rail is going crazy because at long last, they get to take their chilled bones home."

In the annals of Keeneland, this became the shot — and the race — that came down to the wire.

DREAMER

In October 2004, racing fans were taken aback to see a giant sign reading "Keeneland Welcomes the Breeders' Cup" splashed across the entire length of the starting gate. In

Keeneland subbed for Belmont Park for a movie about Secretariat.

George Scott and Colleen Dewhurst meet one of the real stars of Keeneland; opposite, James E. Bassett escorts George Hamilton and Elizabeth Taylor to the winner's circle.

fact, Keeneland has never hosted the event, traditionally run at venues that accommodate 100,000 and more.

"Hollywood knows a good place for a Breeders' Cup," said Nicholson to writer Rich Copley.

When writer-director John Gatins wrote the script for his film *Dreamer*, he described the climactic Breeders' Cup race as being run at "a veritable cathedral of horse racing." "That's exactly what this is," said Gatins of Keeneland. "I've been to many racetracks in North America, and this is definitely the most beautiful in my eyes."

Dreamer: Inspired by a True Story, starring Kurt Russell, Dakota Fanning, Kris Kristofferson, and Elisabeth Shue, is the story of a young girl determined that her trainer father win the Breeders Cup Classic with a horse to whom fortune has been less than kind.

Charming, polite, gregarious, and precocious "in a good way," Dakota Fanning quickly endeared herself to all at Keeneland. Nicholson enjoyed "seeing the kid come out" on a visit to the *Dreamer* set.

"Pleased to meet you, Mr. Nicholson. You have a lovely facility here," said the ten-year-old Fanning solemnly, perched in a director's chair, her feet barely reaching the ground, when they were introduced.

"Then," said Nicholson, "John Gatins pulled four candy bars out of his pocket and said, 'Dakota, I have a problem and I need your advice. I don't know which one would be best to eat first.'

"Quick as a wink, the self-possessed grown-up disappeared and out came a ten-year-old kid with a serious sweet tooth. Her review of each candy bar was precise and accurate, ending with, '… and this one's my favorite.' "

The canny Gatins was happy to share.

SECRETARIAT, THE MAKING OF A CHAMPION

"The beauty of the Keeneland Library," wrote author Laura Hillenbrand, "is that in its magnificent archives, all of racing's greats are immortal, living forever in the supreme moments of their youth." There writer Bill Nack researched *Secretariat: The Making of A Champion*, so it was almost inevitable Keeneland would play a role in the movie based on the bestseller.

On a 40-degree day in September 2009, Keeneland became Belmont Park on an 80-degree day in June. On hand for the filming, Nack invited his old friend, Keeneland's assistant librarian Phyllis Rogers, to be an extra. As stars Diane Lane, as owner Penny Chenery, and John Malkovitch, as trainer Lucien Laurin, watched the horses being saddled in the paddock, Rogers chatted with Secretariat's real-life jockey Ron Turcotte. While confident the silks made for the jockey playing him in the movie were reasonably accurate, Turcotte admitted he couldn't quite remember if they had a bow tie or not and the uncertainty was bothering him.

Hurrying back to the library, Rogers found the famous photograph of Turcotte turning back in the homestretch to see the field an astounding twenty-two lengths behind him, with no trace of a bow tie on his silks. Back on the set, the photo put a thrilled Turcotte's mind at ease. Unfortunately, this proof that the race scenes, already in the can, had been shot with inaccurate silks, had quite the opposite effect on the production designers.

In the classic film *Casablanca*, Rick's Café Americain in Morocco is the crossroads of the world. "Sooner or later, everybody comes to Rick's," observed puckish Captain Renault. And sooner or later, the marquee names in the entertainment industry all seem to come to Keeneland.

Here are a few favorite stories about some household names who, for an afternoon, stepped off the world stage and into the world of racing as it was meant to be. To savor the spectacle and pageantry of what former Keeneland president, trustee, and chairman of the board, James E. (Ted) Bassett III describes as "the show that speaks for itself."

GEORGE C. SCOTT AND COLLEEN DEWHURST

In 1967 George C. Scott delivered one of his most enjoyable performances as a professional con man in *The Flim-Flam Man*, much of which was shot in and around Lexington and Lawrenceburg. Bassett, then head of the Kentucky State Police, had occasion to meet Scott when the police were requested to rope off the roads around Harrodsburg for the filming of a high-speed chase scene. On a day off from the set, Scott and his wife, Colleen Dewhurst, came to Keeneland as guests of Harry Miller, a local attorney they had met at Hollywood Park.

Ashley Judd, with husband Dario Francitti, has made many appearances at Keeneland.

LIZ AND GEORGE

In 1986 Elizabeth Taylor began to be spotted in the playgrounds of the rich and famous on the arm of actor and tanning virtuoso George Hamilton. The globetrotting pair was everywhere: Puerto Vallarta, Acapulco, Gstaad, Rome. And Keeneland.

Marge Everett, owner of Hollywood Park, making the rounds to promote the racetrack as a venue for the Breeders' Cup, brought her friend Liz along on her trip to Central Kentucky to make sure her campaign received the attention it deserved.

"Elizabeth Taylor was stunning. At the top of her game," said Bill Greely. "She and George Hamilton made a striking couple."

"Two words," rhapsodized Bassett. "Gorgeous eyes. Most beautiful I've ever seen. She was all you had hoped she would be."

Miss Taylor agreed to present the Beaumont Stakes Cup, and G.D. Hieronymus, now Keeneland's director of broadcast services, happened to be documenting the event for Hammond Productions. Hearing about Taylor's visit, a friend of Hieronymus begged to be allowed to work on the crew, just to catch a glimpse of his idol in the flesh. The sight of Taylor at the height of her beauty literally transfixed him. So abruptly did he stop in mid-stride that the famous face came perilously close to contact with the camera tripod slung on his shoulder.

Unruffled, the goddess made a minuscule course correction and moved on, a small smile in her eyes. It was obvious, said Hieronymus, she was both accustomed to, and amused by, the effect she had on mere mortals.

CSI CENTRAL KENTUCKY

Jerry Bruckheimer, nicknamed Mr. Blockbuster, is one of the most successful producers of all time. In 2009 his Bruckheimer Films was responsible for six hugely popular television shows, including the *CSI* franchise.

On occasion Bruckheimer brings his creative teams out to the farm he and his wife Linda own in Linda's hometown of Bloomfield, Kentucky. And on occasion they make an afternoon of it at Keeneland.

Nicholson says Jerry Bruckheimer has an aura about him. "You can tell you're in the presence of someone who's very, very good at what he does. He doesn't say much, but you can tell he's taking it all in, soaking it all up, like a sponge."

This assessment was borne out one night as the Nicholsons watched an episode of *CSI Miami* wittily entitled, "And They're Offed." A horse owner is shot in his private luxury suite at a racetrack and the crime is solved because the murder weapon was wrapped in a towel bearing traces of Polytrack TM.

Charlize Theron helps present the trophy for the 2009 Dixiana Breeders' Futurity.

"What's Polytrack?" asks CSI squad investigator Eric Delco.

The answer ("It's cleaner, drains faster and is more animal friendly") "came straight off the Keeneland Web site," said Nicholson.

ASHLEY JUDD AND DARIO FRANCHITTI

One of Nick Nicholson's favorite "Keeneland moments" occurred when actress Ashley Judd brought her husband, race car driver Dario Franchitti, to Keeneland for the first time. Since Franchitti had never watched a horse race live, Nicholson took the two down to the track to watch the horses start.

Franchitti, said Nicholson, was mesmerized. As an athlete himself, he could appreciate both horsepower and strategy. The jockeys, he mused, had it harder than race drivers. Mechanical equipment was predictable to a degree — turn the wheel a fraction and you know what will happen. But a jockey, on a live mount, has no such certainty.

Taking him to the jockeys' room after the race, Nicholson smiled to see a group of men, for the first time in his experience, mob Franchitti rather than his fetching wife. Comparing notes about the hazards of their respective professions, both jockeys and racecar driver were in perfect agreement about what topped the list. "A bad jockey," said Pat Day. "A bad driver," said Franchitti.

Says Nicholson, "I got to be an observer of a genuine connection, a unique meeting of minds, between two groups of athletes both specializing, in different ways, in harnessing horsepower."

CHARLIZE THERON

Oscar-winning actress Charlize Theron made an unexpected appearance at the Keeneland fall meet in 2009. As the guest of Dixiana Farm owner and film producer William Shively, Theron helped present the trophy for the grade I Breeders' Futurity, sponsored by Dixiana Farms. A passionate animal-rights activist and supporter of People for the Ethical Treatment of Animals, Theron appeared to succumb to the sheer excitement and spectacle, reportedly surprising even herself by placing a bet.

In *Casablanca*, Rick Blaine says to Captain Renault as the plane carrying Ilsa Lund and Victor Lazlo disappears into the night sky, "Louis. I think this is the beginning of a beautiful friendship."

Keeneland cherishes the beautiful friendship forged over the years between the silver screen and the sport of kings. What has brought Hollywood to Keeneland is the intangible magic that lies behind the simple ivy-framed sign that says Keeneland Race Course. The old-fashioned beauty of the facility, the ivy-wreathed stone gently touched by time, the towering trees, the rolling green vistas, the demeanor and dress of the fans, the minutely observed rites and rituals, the discreet good taste, the respect for tradition, the genteel pageantry of it all.

And it is this star quality that will keep it coming back, as time goes by.

LIFE ON THE BACKSTRETCH

MARYJEAN WALL

Dawn slips into Keeneland on pastel folds of velvet clouds: skylight blues and peach-toned pinks that linger, then disappear behind the brilliant globe of an orange sun rising. Here at this hour, when electric light gives way to daylight, a community of horses, pets, and people is a thriving city of activity. On any day at any time of year, this backstretch community has been at work for two, perhaps three hours before commuter traffic builds nearby on Versailles Road.

The barn area is the heart and soul of any racetrack. During the early morning hours, a workforce at Keeneland that varies from perhaps 100 persons in the off-season to 1,200 or more during the race meets goes about its seven-day-a-week routine of caring for the needs of racehorses. Backstretch workers fill a variety of roles: from trainers, assistant trainers, barn foremen, grooms, and hotwalkers, to private-practice veterinarians, representatives for tack stores, feed companies, and hay suppliers, jockey agents, equine physical therapists, farriers, horse van drivers, EMTs in case of accidents on the track, equine ambulance crews, and racing commission veterinarians to inspect the horses entered to race that day. Keeneland's backstretch is unique in North America, for the racing association permits the public to stroll through the barn area to observe activities. Visitor traffic is always highest on weekends during the race meets, particularly on Saturday mornings following the popular trackside program "Breakfast with the Works."

On any morning, visitors will encounter horses with their riders up, walking to and from the main track or the training track. During most of the year one or both of these tracks is open from 6 a.m. until 10 a.m., although times might vary during the winter. Trainers of these horses will watch them take their exercise, observing from the grandstand, on horseback, or standing by the rail. Throughout the year Keeneland hosts the stables of a wide variety of trainers, from Hall of Famers like Jonathan Sheppard, Nick Zito, Bill Mott, and Carl Nafzger to trainers whose stables are frequently in the news, like Todd Pletcher and Steve Asmussen. A small number of trainers keep their stables year-round at the

Racehorses receive meticulous care, from bathing to grooming to new shoes.

Leg wraps, which protect racehorse's delicate limbs, dry in the morning sun.

Keeneland Training Center on Rice Road. Some stables serve as divisions of larger stables, preparing young horses for their racing careers; others follow the seasonal racing circuits or ship horses to race at regional tracks, returning them to their Keeneland barns following individual races.

Trainers occupy the highest level of the career ladder in any racing stable. Trainers map out racing campaigns for horses in their charge. They closely watch the progress in their horses' training to know whether the animals are on schedule for racing; frequently, adjustments must be made because training is an art as well as a science. Trainers in large operations delegate various functions to their assistant trainers or barn foremen such as overseeing the work of employees, negotiating race-riding engagements with jockeys, and conferring with veterinarians. During the meets, the trainer or the assistant trainer saddles the stable's horses for racing and issues riding instructions to the jockey.

The trainer also consults with the owners of these horses. Some trainers operate their own businesses, known as public stables; others work privately and under contract for farms or individuals.

Back at the barns in the mornings, horses spend most of their time in the company of their grooms and hotwalkers. The latter walk the horses around the shed rows of the barns or around outdoor rings to cool them out after exercise. The job of a hotwalker is entry-level, the position at which the majority of barn workers begin their careers. Many Hall-of-Fame jockeys and trainers started out as hotwalkers.

The work of the groom is much more complex and higher on the scale of jobs than hotwalker. As once described in *Sports Illustrated*, grooms are "men and women who make and remake the straw beds in the horses' stalls, who wake up at early light to care for the animals, who turn off the lights at night for them, who scold and succor and curry them. Who brush, rub, massage, bathe, hose, sponge, feed, water, stroke, graze and bandage them. Who pick their feet and sing to them. Who mix their mash and fill their racks with hay. Who dose their feed with thick liquid vitamin mix, pouring it on the oats like syrup over pancakes. Who take the horses' temperatures, paint their feet, feel for hot spots in their ankles and knees. Who swab their legs with poultices of medicated mud and stand the horses for hours in tubs of ice. Who lead them to the wars and back."

To say that Keeneland's backstretch operates like a small city is not too much of an exaggeration. Barn workers have at their disposal social services, church services, recreational activities,

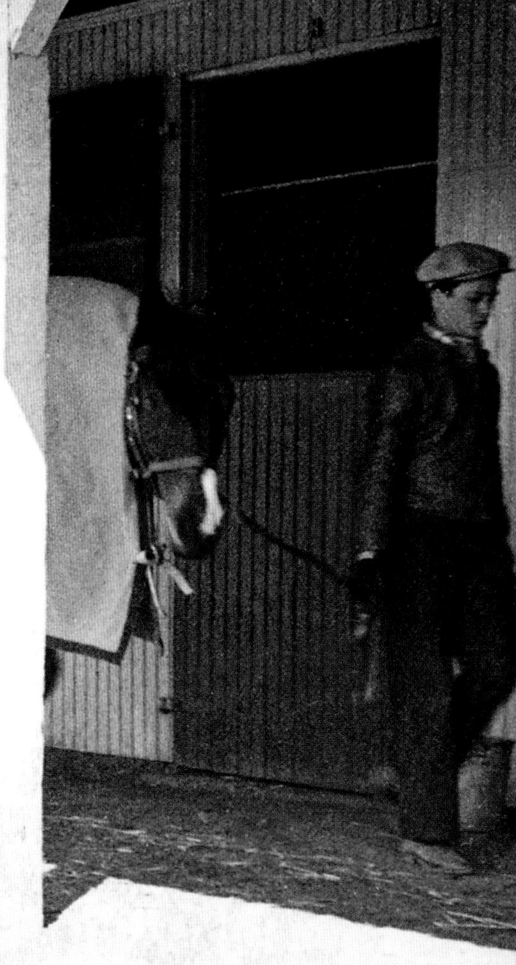

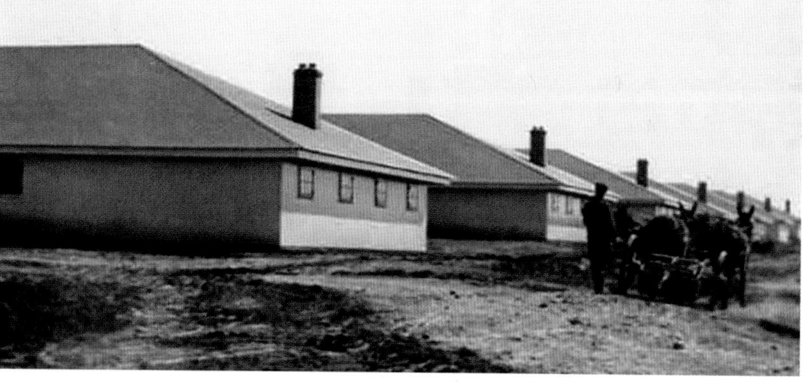

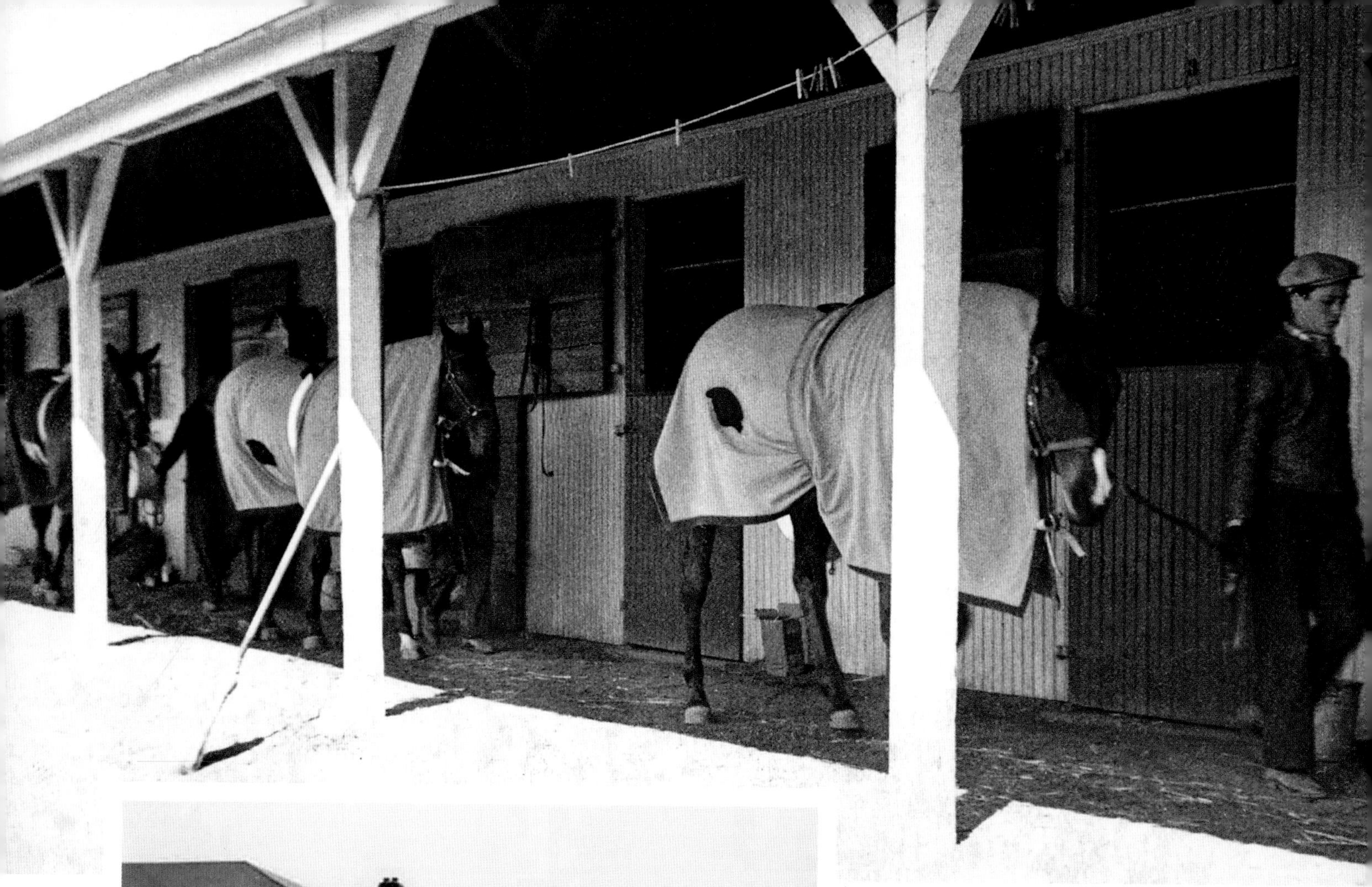

Top, racehorses get cooled out walking the shed row of one of Keeneland's early barns; above, a mule team works to ready the barn area in 1936.

food services, transportation services, and housing. The backstretch even has the appearance of a small city, or at least a village, with people walking in and out of numbered barns and along interior roads laid out in grids. If you know your way around you'll know instantly where you can find barn thirty-five or barn forty-two. The numbering system is of immense help to veterinarians, jockeys, feed dealers making deliveries, and anyone wishing to locate a particular stable. Individual stalls within each barn also are numbered; in effect, each horse in residence has its own address.

The Keeneland backstretch is renowned for its aesthetic beauty. Trees shade every barn and no barn is without access to an adjacent, outdoor walking ring. During afternoons, grooms often graze their horses on lawns between the barns — another horse amenity unique to Keeneland. Horse trainers have often remarked on the value of this benefit. For example, the late Hall of Fame trainer Horatio Luro told how he relied on the restorative qualities of Keeneland's spring grass in preparing for his two Kentucky Derby victories, in 1962 with Decidedly and in 1964 with Northern Dancer. In Decidedly's year, Luro hired an extra man whose sole duty was to graze the colt at Keeneland: two hours in the morning and another two in the afternoon. Luro believed that the spring air at Keeneland, combined with the fresh grass, put the finishing touches on his colts to enable them to win the Derby.

Visitors to the backstretch observe a vastly different landscape than existed when the track opened for its inaugural meet in the autumn of 1936. Most remarkable is the number of barns: the Keeneland backstretch has five times as many as it had for that first race meet, when only thirteen barns were in place. The number of barns during the first decade of the twenty-first century totaled fifty-eight. Forty-nine barns used for housing horses are situated on the main property, along with a "detention barn" designated for drug-testing following races. Nine additional barns are located at the Keeneland Training Center adjacent to the back portion of the racecourse. The year-round equine population occupies the training center barns, while barns on the main property generally are reserved for race meets and sales. Keeneland also maintains a barn for quarantine of newly arrived horses from offshore.

Keeneland has gone from 13 to 58 barns; below, the backside bustles on race days.

Keeneland's first general manager, the late W. T. Bishop, once told how the racing association was fortunate to acquire construction material from an abandoned racetrack, which helped in keeping costs reasonable. Thus as the new track went under construction, Keeneland acquired lumber for barns from the century-old Kentucky Association track in Lexington's east end, at Fifth and Race streets, which had closed in 1933. According

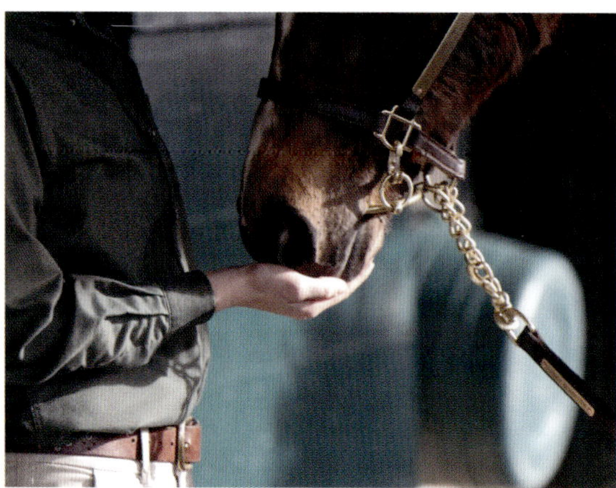

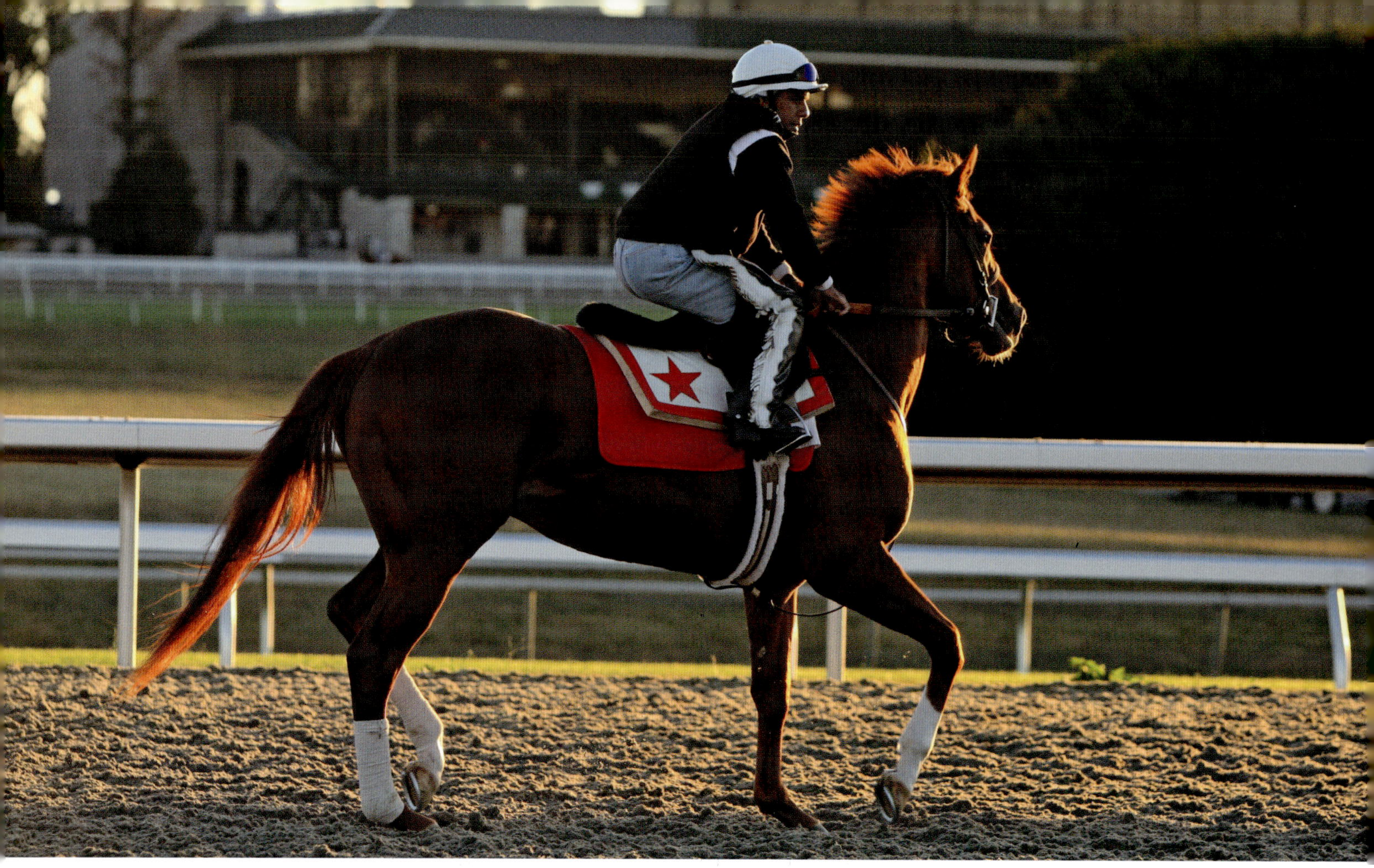

Opposite, some spirited racehorses benefit from stable companions such as goats; opposite, right, the original track kitchen featured a neon sign at the entrance.

to Bishop's recollections, Keeneland purchased framing and roofing from five of the old track's barns for about $150 to $200 apiece.

The backstretch has changed in other ways since the inaugural race meet. Twenty-first century veterinarians can be seen driving through the barn area in vehicles, usually SUVs, packed with state-of-the-art diagnostic equipment in addition to the customary array of equine medications. Some veterinarians include acupuncture and equine chiropractic treatments among their specialties. Besides veterinarians, those making the rounds of barns include equine physical therapists. This field did not exist when Keeneland first opened; physical therapists entered racing in small numbers during the late 1970s and slowly gained acceptance in the backstretch community. Their equipment runs a gamut from lasers to deep muscle massage machines, similar to what would be seen in a sports medicine facility for humans. Horses are athletes in training and benefit from these therapeutic modalities in the same way human athletes do from similar treatments.

While Keeneland does not have a horse surgery facility on-site, three major equine hospitals are located within a short van drive from the track. Thus, Keeneland's backstretch is linked with veterinary care that owners, trainers, and veterinarians acknowledge worldwide as premier in the horse world.

One thing that has not changed through the years at Keeneland is the commitment to the Thoroughbred racehorse. Backstretch workers form emotional bonds with the horses they care for; the horse is central to their workday and often to their lives. "It's all about the horse," said a career outrider and former trainer and jockey, Susan Shurtleff. "It's early in the morning and you're on a wonderful horse. It's just you and the horse: power, speed, and the excitement of being at the races."

In this specialized world, citizens of the backstretch incorporate the horse into their most memorable moments. At Keeneland-owned Turfway Park, when it was known as Latonia, a backstretch wedding once took place only hours before the evening's races. The wedding chapel was set up in the "receiving barn" where horses ship in for the races from off-track stabling. Those who attended, all of them backstretch workers, sat on bales of straw laid out like church pews in the aisle of the barn. More straw bales were piled atop one another to form an altar. Six jockeys clad in racing silks comprised the attendants. The racetrack chaplain married the couple. The congregation shivered

because the temperature dipped to frigid on the thermometer. But at the reception that followed in the track kitchen, everyone warmed up while feasting on punch, peanuts, and popcorn.

While the backstretch is all about horses and people, it's also about stable pets. Goats used to fill major roles in racing barns, where their job was to baby-sit extremely nervous horses. Goat numbers have declined, possibly because physical therapy and acupuncture can achieve similar, calming effects. Cats remain ubiquitous, however, for they always have and probably always will serve as the most effective rodent control in racetrack barns.

At one time, Keeneland was home to a track kitchen cat that just happened to be named for then Keeneland president James E. "Ted" Bassett III. Teddy Bassett the cat came "skin and bones" to the racecourse after one spring race meet, as the cat's human namesake once described the animal. However, the cat soon fattened up. He lived in a sturdy little wooden "cat house" that Keeneland maintenance workers constructed for him and placed at the front door of the kitchen. Another cat named Midnight lived at the back door of the same building. Keeneland's president, whose custom was to take his breakfast every morning in the track kitchen, had a special fondness for the cat that shared his name. He also got a kick out of people calling, "Here, Teddy; here, Teddy." When Teddy I disappeared one day never to return, another cat soon moved in to occupy the little house, as is the habit of stray cats. Kitchen regulars named the new occupant, "Teddy II."

Almost inevitably, visitors to the Keeneland backstretch find their way to the track kitchen. In fact the track kitchen, or cafeteria, is world-famous for its biscuits and gravy and other "country" meals, served in the ambience of a congenial racing community. Only in the track kitchen will you find horse owners taking their breakfast with exercise riders, jockey agents, and various others whose tales of the turf, whether true or not, keep everyone entertained.

Turf Catering has long operated the kitchen. During the 1970s, before Turf Catering took over the job, the late Wally Cox was the cafeteria's proprietor. Cox was an accomplished chef who also liked to bet the horses. Unfortunately for him, he wasn't very good at it

Opposite, the Keeneland Kitchen is famous for its biscuits and gravy and other hearty fare.

— his betting habits kept him in hot water as often as he boiled water in his duties as chef. For a brief time, Cox attempted to draw people from town on Sunday by offering sumptuous brunches, $5 per person, and which rivaled clubhouse fare in quality. Brunch included six meats, twelve salads, eight or nine vegetables, pastries, fresh fruit, gelatin, and a beverage. The price included tax and tips. Brunch became so popular that patrons lined up at the kitchen waiting for the door to open, wearing everything from blue jeans to their Sunday best.

The present-day track kitchen is at least the second to exist at Keeneland. Today's track kitchen, with more than 6,800 square feet of floor space, seats 120 persons in two wings. The former kitchen, which existed into the 1970s, also had two wings and a clientele that followed a seating pattern held over from the segregation era, long after this era had

Farriers, exercise riders, feed people, and others ply their trade on the backside.

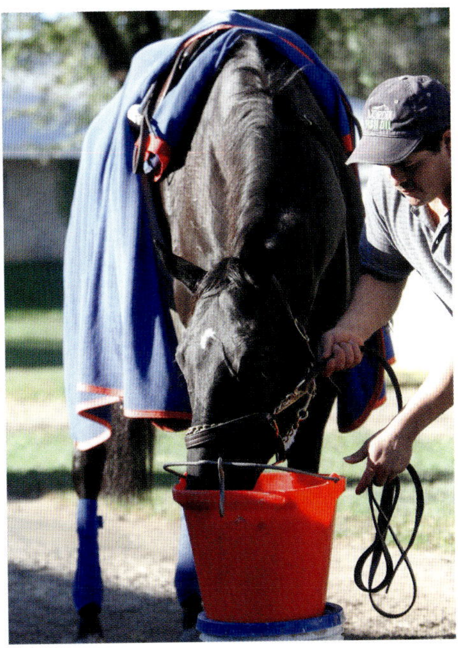

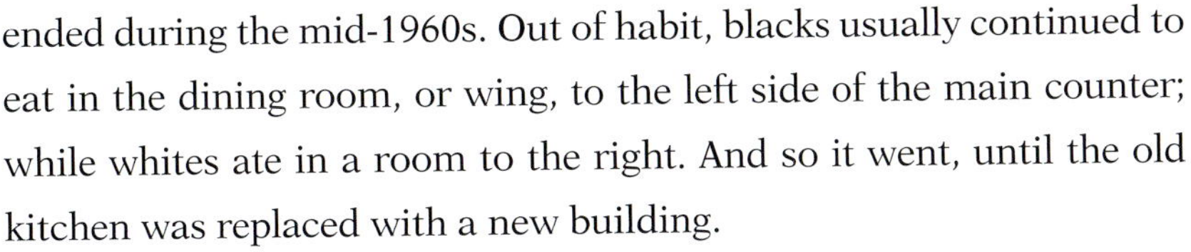

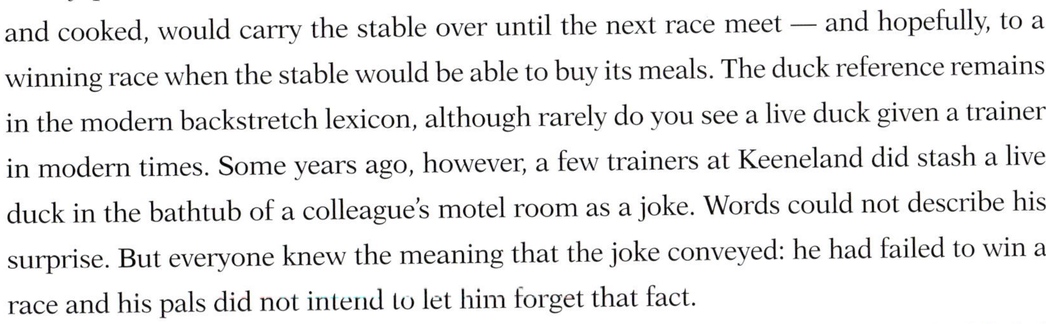

ended during the mid-1960s. Out of habit, blacks usually continued to eat in the dining room, or wing, to the left side of the main counter; while whites ate in a room to the right. And so it went, until the old kitchen was replaced with a new building.

For any racetracker, a meal holds great importance. In fact a meal on the wing holds as much significance as a hearty meal taken in the track kitchen. Herein lies an introduction to racetrack lore: when backstretch folk speak of "getting the duck" they refer to the live duck that traditionally was presented to the trainer who failed to win a race at any particular meet. The idea was that the duck, when plucked and cooked, would carry the stable over until the next race meet — and hopefully, to a winning race when the stable would be able to buy its meals. The duck reference remains in the modern backstretch lexicon, although rarely do you see a live duck given a trainer in modern times. Some years ago, however, a few trainers at Keeneland did stash a live duck in the bathtub of a colleague's motel room as a joke. Words could not describe his surprise. But everyone knew the meaning that the joke conveyed: he had failed to win a race and his pals did not intend to let him forget that fact.

Trainer Doug Davis received a duck at Keeneland one autumn because he had failed to win a race. His experience epitomized that racetrack colloquialism of "chicken today, feathers tomorrow" — and vice-versa. The following year Keeneland awarded Davis a silver julep cup for his standing as the track's then-all-time leading trainer. Such are the ups and downs of life on the backstretch. This story would have been told and retold in the track kitchen, to the amusement of many.

Racetrack lore, those tales of the turf retold many times over in the track kitchen, is often spun in jargon not readily grasped by the outside world. Citizens of the backstretch

have developed their own language that runs a gamut of words and phrases like "acey ducey" (a riding style of left stirrup lower than the right to give a jockey better balance in the turns), "cast, or casted" (when a horse becomes immobilized, caught with its legs pinned against the wall of its stall), "climbing" (a horse's running style or way of handling a track surface, making the leg action abnormally high), "hands" (a unit of measurement for equine height: one hand equals four inches), and "on the bit" (a horse's eagerness to run expressed by leaning fully into the bit and bridle). At least, this was the common language when grooms and various other backstretch habitués went by names like Bananas, Duck Butter, Slow and Easy, Hamburger, and Roadrunner.

The nicknames and lexicon have changed radically since the influx of Hispanics into the racetrack workforce, a seismic demographic change that took hold in the latter 1980s. The backstretch generally has reflected changes in the larger society but the arrival of Hispanics at racetrack barns might have occurred ahead of the curve seen in the general population in the United States. Single men arrived first, speaking little or no English and seeking entry-level jobs. Many of their numbers learned the language and moved up the career ladder to become barn foremen or assistant trainers. Then they brought their families to live in Lexington or surrounding Bluegrass towns. Now in the twenty-first century, Hispanic men and women comprise the majority of the workforce in nearly every racing stable.

Magdaleno Nolazco, who is from Michoacan, Mexico, represents not only this Hispanic turn in the workforce but also the international diversity at Keeneland. When interviewed

Horses cross Rice Road en route to train with assistance from a crossing guard.

for this book, Nolazco was working as an assistant trainer in the Darley operation of Sheikh Mohammed bin Rashid al Maktoum, ruler of Dubai. Darley maintains a year-round barn at Keeneland under Irish-born trainer John Burke, who is one of numerous trainers employed in the Sheikh's worldwide racing operation. At Keeneland, one can easily see the microcosm of this dynamic: the Hispanic working for the Irish working for the ruling Sheikh of Dubai.

Nolazco has come far since arriving in the United States during 1981. His job description of assistant trainer means he is in charge if Burke, the Irish trainer, is away from the barn for any reason. Nolazco said he has found an increasing number of opportunities since his first trip from Mexico. Initially, he worked with racehorses in California and in New York and found his existence in this country challenging. He did not speak English. He relied on a dictionary for his first seven years and recalled, "You try to learn little by little."

The language problem that non-Spanish speaking trainers deal with is, according to John Ward, a lifelong Kentucky horseman who trained the 2001 Kentucky Derby

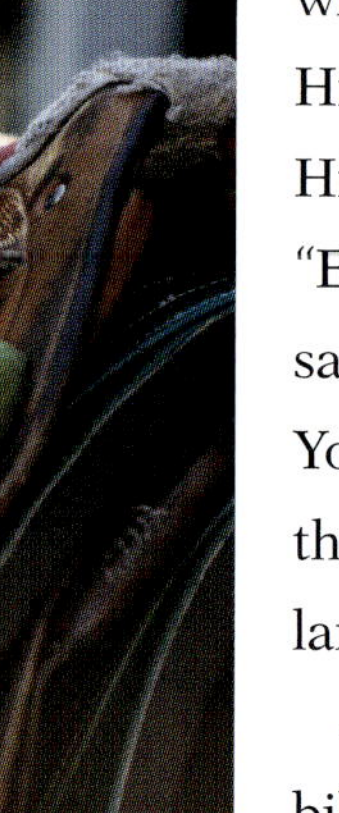

winner, Monarchos, the greatest challenge he has faced in employing Hispanic workers. Moreover, he has learned from his experience that Hispanics represent a variety of cultures and geographic origins. "Everybody wants to put Hispanics into one neat little bowl," Ward said. "But there are Guatemalans, Nicaraguans, Mexicans, Peruvians. You can't put them together. You've got to understand how they mix, that there are undercurrents there. Just because they speak the same language doesn't mean they all get along."

As Hispanics from earlier immigration waves, like Nolazco, became bilingual they became invaluable on the backstretch as translators for

newer waves of immigrants. Many have also become citizens of the Bluegrass region, enrolling their children in local schools and planning to remain in the United States.

Hispanics have turned the backstretch into more of a family workplace, with wives working alongside husbands. A similar phenomenon has emerged among American-born horsemen. Trainers including John and Donna Ward and Larry and Cindy Jones are husbands and wives who have worked alongside each other to operate some of the most recognizable training operations in North America. This is a noticeable departure from previous decades when only men ran the major racing operations.

John Ward has witnessed backstretch demographics change since previous generations when his father, John Ward, and uncle, Sherrill Ward, operated racing stables. He believes that in this respect the backstretch has reflected larger society. "A backside (another word for backstretch) usually reflects whatever the abundance of the labor is at that particular moment in the economy," Ward said. "Back in the 1940s and '50s it was the all-American backside, a mix of black and white."

A wave of women to the backstretch during the 1960s and 1970s diversified the workforce from its all-male population. Donna Ward was among these women, working originally as an exercise rider in the John Ward stable and later as a trainer in that

operation. Among horses she trained was champion Beautiful Pleasure. She recalled that when women initially began working as exercise riders in the late 1960s and early 1970s, "It was a novelty. They were girls who loved to ride but distanced themselves from the real backside."

As women came to Thoroughbred racing in greater numbers, their novelty diminished. The sport became more accepting of women jockeys and trainers, although by the twenty-first century their numbers still do not compete with those of men. Nonetheless Donna Ward felt compelled when interviewed in 2009 to say, "It would be hard for me to imagine the backside being able to run without women. So many women are now foremen. They're organized. They're meticulous. And you see a lot of husband-and-wife teams. You see wives riding the horses for husbands or they run the barns for them."

As the backstretch has evolved through the years, so has Keeneland's commitment to the workforce of the barn area. The most noticeable change has been the dormitory, built in two phases, to house workers who choose to live close to the horses. The first phase, completed in 1987, included forty-four sleeping rooms; the second, completed in 1999, added another thirty-four rooms for a total of seventy-eight. This represented a huge step forward from previous living accommodations. Traditional housing was limited to

the tack rooms located along the ends of each barn, where grooms placed their cots. In 1950 Keeneland also opened a second-floor sleeping loft over the top of a maintenance building. The loft had room to accommodate twenty-four men: grooms, exercise riders, and van drivers. Those accommodations no longer exist.

Keeneland also works closely with the Kentucky Thoroughbred Association (KTA) and the Horsemen's Benevolent and Protective Association (HBPA) to provide backstretch workers with health care, recreational opportunities, and education. According to Michael Powers, the track chaplain for ten years, Keeneland and the Kentucky Racetrack Chaplaincy provide GED and ESL classes. Backstretch workers also have access to health-care foundation money through the Kentucky Racing Health and Welfare Fund, the Kentucky Thoroughbred Association, and the Horsemen's Benevolent and Protective Association. Medical care, dental work, optical care, and medications are provided to backstretch workers at little or no cost. The chaplaincy holds weekly non-denominational services, one in English and another in Spanish. A room where workers can select from gently worn clothing is located in the dormitory.

Also situated inside the dormitory building is the Keeneland Learning Center which contains a computer lab. Backstretch employees have access to counseling for substance abuse. They benefit from an annual health fair held in conjunction with a Thanksgiving dinner. A cancer-screening event is also held at the track. The Jockey Club and *The Thoroughbred Times* co-sponsor a Christmas party. Claudio Toro, a chaplain who speaks Spanish fluently, assists the Rev. Powers at the track as well as serving the Blue Grass Farms Chaplaincy, which provides similar services to horse farm workers.

But for all the changes through the years, one constant on the Keeneland backstretch has remained the horse. And most backstretch workers will say that their most enjoyable times spent in the company of a horse are in the early mornings. Spectacular sunrises over the tops of roof barns remain as special to those who take notice in modern times as they must have been when the track opened in 1936. Peach and pink and skylight blue torn to bright orange rising on the horizon. Another dawn arrives at Keeneland. Somewhere, a horse whinnies.

KEENELAND AND INNOVATION

RICK BAILEY

Racing as it was meant to be. Keeneland's motto for years has captured the essence of the sport conducted in the center of the Thoroughbred world for three-quarters of a century. The changing seasons of spring and autumn are still presented in a gorgeous arrangement. The horses still train in the mornings and race in the afternoons.

And yet racing has witnessed major changes in the first decade of the twenty-first century. What racing was meant to be has entered a bold, new world.

Instead of watching this ever-changing environment surge over them, Keeneland's leaders have placed themselves on the cutting edge by embracing new technology, meeting the challenges of customer service, and never wavering from their founders' creed that the horse must always come first.

In 2006 Keeneland became the first U.S. racetrack to use Polytrack on its main track.

Former Keeneland president James E. "Ted" Bassett III, in his 2009 autobiography with collaborator Bill Mooney, wrote that the track had been branded, sometimes erroneously, as conservative, stodgy, and resistant to change. Rather, they wrote, "Keeneland has long been an innovator and views the past as a guidepost rather than a hitching post."

Some Thoroughbred fans were convinced that sweeping changes in the new order would turn Keeneland into "racing as it is everywhere else," as one headline put it.

Fans instead have welcomed innovations such as Trakus video race technology. Owners have accepted Polytrack, the all-weather racing surface, for its safety features and consistency, especially for training. Consignors and buyers at Keeneland's annual auctions now have access to a state-of-the-art digital repository for their veterinarians to examine a horse's medical records and X-rays. Keeneland was the first to stream live sales sessions throughout the world via the Internet beginning in 2000.

BID BOARD

An enthralled audience could only watch in amazement as the numbers on the bid board climbed at mostly $100,000 increments during the 1983 July select yearling sale.

Robert Sangster and his partners in the British Bloodstock Agency were bidding against Sheikh Mohammed bin Rashid al Maktoum for Hip No. 308, a colt by Northern Dancer.

"When the bidding reached $10 million, all that showed up on our bid board was a line of zeros," wrote then Keeneland president James E. "Ted" Bassett III in his 2009 autobiography co-written with Bill Mooney. "This brought a gasp from the people sitting in the pavilion. Was that a bid? Well, no, the problem was that our board only went to seven digits."

When the sheikh raised what would be the final bid, the board showed $200,000. Auctioneer Tom Caldwell informed the packed pavilion that the bid actually was $10.2 million, and soon his hammer fell on a then record-priced yearling.

Needless to say, an extra digit was placed on the board following the sale.

Nick Nicholson, current president and CEO, recognized the perception of Keeneland as a track bound by tradition. He is pleased with the new age that has burst on the scene in recent years.

"One of those traditions has been a willingness to adapt to new technology," he said. "Instead of being among the last, Keeneland has been among the first in moving forward. We have been true to our tradition of embracing technology to make the customer experience better."

During his first decade at the helm, Nicholson put together a team of experienced experts already on site and talented newcomers to meet the challenges of the information age. For instance, Brad Lovell, who grew up in Lexington, came from NASCAR to become Keeneland's director of information technology in 2009.

Keeneland Association also has enjoyed a long and valued alliance with The Jockey Club, which over the years developed Equibase and revolutionized operations in the racing office.

Behind-the-scenes technology has enriched the wagering experience (if not the pocket books) of the betting public. Compare the thick, magazine-sized race day program to the 4-by-9-inch program of the past.

A look around the historic track constantly reveals racing as it is today and offers hints of what it might become in the future.

'A SWEET THING TO RUN OVER'

Keeneland officials were beaming on October 6, 2006, when a new, all-weather synthetic racing surface — Polytrack — made its successful debut. Most trainers and jockeys hailed the change. "I think Polytrack is a great thing," trainer Kenny McPeek said that day. "The problem before ... was the limestone base. It was hard on the horses. (Polytrack) is so forgiving. It's like a cushion for them, a sweet thing to run over."

Race Announcer / KURT BECKER

After he made history with the first live race call from Keeneland, Kurt Becker found himself on the elevator with noted horseman Cot Campbell of Dogwood Stable.

"So you're the young man Keeneland hired," Campbell said. "We couldn't understand a thing you said."

"He was referring to the level of the audio," Becker remembered from that day. "In a way I was relieved."

At the same time, according to the *Daily Racing Form*, Becker gave himself a C- for his first day as Keeneland's race announcer on April 6, 1997.

Becker, then twenty-seven, was the choice of Keeneland president Bill Greely from more than forty applicants to become the track's first public address announcer.

Dismissive of a P.A. system, one of the track's founders reportedly said that patrons knew enough to identify the horses by their silks.

Keeneland remained the only track in the United States without an on-track announcer

The engineered synthetic top layer is composed of recycled polypropylene fibers, recycled rubber, and silica sand. Components are weighed, mixed, and coated with wax. The coating prevents moisture absorption, allowing water to flow through the top surface into a vertical drainage system.

The layers include loose Polytrack (about three inches), compact Polytrack (about seven inches), porous macadam (asphalt), clean stone, and dense grade aggregate rock. A system of perforated drainage pipes forms the underground drainage system.

Keeneland spent five years of research, planning, and construction before it became the third North American track (behind subsidiary Turfway Park in Northern Kentucky and Woodbine in Canada) to go "Poly" with designs of preventing horses' breakdowns and jockeys' injuries. The only breakdown of the first meet came on the last day.

Rogers Beasley, director of racing, championed the idea of an artificial surface. Along

> **A sixty-year tradition was laid to rest when Becker got the call.**

even though it had a P.A. system for calling inter-track wagering races.

A sixty-year tradition was laid to rest when Becker got the call.

As he awaited his debut at Keeneland, he heeded a request from Greely to arrive in Lexington the Monday before, spend the week walking the grounds, and get used to the surroundings.

"He knew that the ambiance of Keeneland is such that even when there was no live racing, it would soak in on me," Becker said. "I was here not to be on center stage. I was here to blend in and be part of the atmosphere. He got his point across."

Becker already had an idea that Keeneland was unique.

In 1988 he would listen to the feature race of the day on his way to calling races at Louisville Downs, a now defunct harness racing track. John Henderson was the anchor and Mike Battaglia called the race.

"It came across with the enthusiasm in their voices that Keeneland was a special place," Becker said. "They painted a picture very well."

Becker follows two creeds when painting his own picture: be clear and be accurate. The stretch call is vital. "Even if things are awkward to that point, if you get things pulled together for the stretch run, you're usually all right," he said.

With bettors playing exotics like the "tri" and superfecta, Becker needs to call not only the winner correctly but also the top three or four finishers.

The feature race is critical, too, because the stretch call gets exposure on TV and radio. "You don't want to have a train wreck at any point," he said, "but that stretch call gets repeated."

Becker also has maintained his position with NASCAR's Motor Racing Network. He works a schedule from about Memorial Day through Labor Day as an announcer for Sprint Cup races and the Nationwide and truck series.

Becker also shares the announcer duties with Henderson during Keeneland's four annual Thoroughbred auctions.

Installion of Poly-track involved several stages, with placement of the surface material, above, one of the last steps in the process.

with maintenance superintendent Mike Young, he visited Lingfield Park in England to examine the new racing and training surface, which offers high performance and low maintenance.

"It rained one day, never let up," Young recalled. "You looked at the track and couldn't tell it was wet. You knew water was there, but it was going out so fast. Polytrack is consistent. We've never had an off track."

Keeneland took up its five-furlong dirt training track in 2004 and replaced it with Polytrack, giving trainers several months to monitor their horses on the artificial surface.

"We wanted to test Polytrack through the four seasons and get the reaction from trainers and exercise riders," Beasley said. "They could kick it around and pick it up. We also wanted to see how the horses reacted to it.

"It was definitely a plus for our racetrack with the kind of changing weather we have. We were patient with Polytrack, and it paid off."

While bettors often have scratched their heads trying to handicap Polytrack, the surface gets high marks for horse and rider safety. The rate of Thoroughbred fatalities at Keeneland is 1.01 per 1,000 starts on Polytrack. The rate is 2.03 on dirt.

Keeneland long has been concerned with the care of horses and jockeys. An inside, aluminum rail replaced the wooden rail in 1949 and was the first of its kind at an American racetrack. The Fontana Safety Rail came along in 1983 and was designed to help cushion a fallen horse or jockey. Rider Protection, a new rail installed in 2006, holds up better with the weather conditions at Keeneland, according to Young.

Starting gate padding was added in 2000 to absorb force when a horse acts up. "Anything

FIRST POLYTRACK RACE

How special was the first Polytrack race at Keeneland?

Lordly, a 31-1 outsider, won the race for three-year-olds and up and returned $65.20, $13, and $8.80. The three-year-old filly edged the favorite Maizelle by a neck.

"It was better than winning the Derby with all the family history," said owner-breeder Louis Lee Haggin III, a longtime Keeneland director and trustee. "It goes back three generations."

Alma, his mother, was a daughter of Keeneland co-founder and first president Hal Price Headley and the wife of Louis Lee Haggin II, who succeeded his father-in-law as president and later was chairman of the board.

"To pop up and win the first race on our artificial track made for a very exciting day," Haggin III said. "She never won another race."

a jockey could feel was padded and so much softer," Young said. Starter Robert "Spec" Alexander added, "If there's any angle in the gate, it's covered up."

TRAKUS TRACKS THE HORSES

On that landmark day in October 2006, Trakus went into operation. Keeneland was the first U.S. track to use the video race technology. The goal was to provide fans with more precise racing coverage and information, according to G.D. Hieronymus, director of broadcast services.

With sensor chips in saddlecloths and antennas around the oval, the system tracks each horse electronically and digitally in real time. Screens display tiles (or "chicklets") and animated horses, their running order, and placement on the track.

Sensor chips placed in the saddle towel enable the precise tracking of a horse during each phase of a race.

"We think this is one of our greatest assets," Beasley said. "It's easier to see where your horse is."

The future for Trakus is wide open, he added. "Australia has put chips in horses for identification. That would be great from the sales standpoint. And all workouts could be electronically timed."

Hieronymus also pushed High-definition technology, which was implemented in 2008.

Directing fifteen HD cameras is the focal point of the video room above the press box where more than twenty people monitor what is happening down below.

TECHNOLOGY ENTERS THE SALES RING

Senior auctioneer Ryan Mahan's chant reverberates through the sales pavilion as another Thoroughbred enters the ring. The staccato beat triggers memories of a past time when yearlings sold for record prices and the bidding between competing buyers was high drama indeed.

The worldwide economic collapse, high stallion fees, and an oversupply of yearlings have stung the sales' industry in recent years. Nevertheless, Keeneland continues to pursue the latest in computer-generated technology. In fact, technology is at the forefront of the

Radiographs and other health information about sale horses are available for review in the repository.

leading revenue producer for the association.

While yearlings proceed through the sales' ring, Central Kentucky veterinarians have been utilizing a "gift" from technology — the digital repository. Standard film X-rays of a horse's legs have been supplanted by thirty-six digital images available for checkout and use at computer stations. Keeneland was the first to offer them worldwide in November 2006.

Beasley, director of sales at the time, and Cathy Schenck, Keeneland's head librarian, launched the repository in 1996. Three trailers housed the first "home." One was for processing and administration, and two served as viewing stations.

Veterinarians now take a portable unit into the field, get their images, view them immediately on a monitor, and put them on a CD. In the repository, sets of digital images are filed by hip number.

G.D.Hieronymus, director of broacast services, oversaw the transition to all HD broadcast.

The process was expensive at the start, but costs have become more manageable and worthwhile to sellers and their veterinarians.

Video endoscopy of a Thoroughbred's airways has drawn attention, according to Lexington veterinarian Craig Van Balen.

"Endoscopy has changed a lot recently," he said. "An exercise rider can strap on a backpack with a battery, take the racehorse out on the track, and get pictures of his upper airways as he's being exercised."

The scope is in the horse's nose during the work. Afterward, a chip is removed from the machine and examined.

Another advance is a hand-held device that looks like a spatula on a handle. It has a small endoscope capable of recording on a digital card.

"We've added new things with each sale," Schenck said, referring to an expansive renovation of the sales pavilion and repository in 2005. "We try to expedite the process for everybody."

Going digital has had a major impact on the auction experience, according to director of sales Geoffrey Russell. "That's from the online entry system through the selling

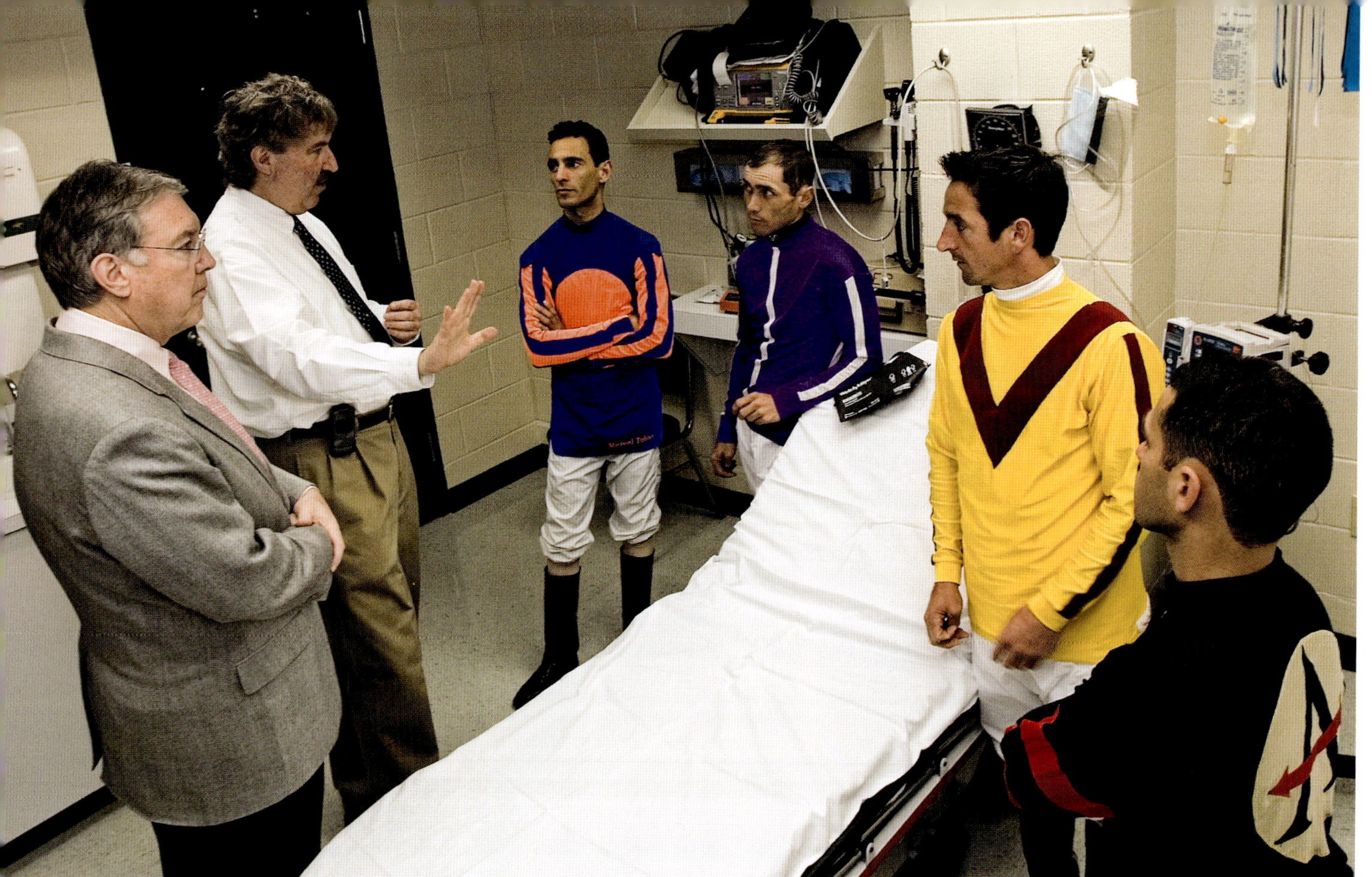

Dr. Barry Schumer, second from left, explains the Jockey Health Infomation System to Keeneland riders.

process," he said. "Sessions can be watched on the Internet around the world, and that's very popular.

"Everything we do has an IT function to it. Getting the proper paperwork can be a nightmare when you're selling thousands of horses. In the old days, there weren't enough file cabinets to keep track of things, but with the digital repository and online entries, life is easier."

Keeneland's Web site is one of its most important marketing tools, Russell said. "There is so much information up there to help consignors and buyers get a step ahead."

Russell can hardly imagine the future awaiting Thoroughbred auctions. "Every day something comes up that we think about," he said. "How we get our message out to different people changes constantly ... Facebook, Twitter, YouTube. As new technology is introduced we're happy to embrace it if it's useful to us."

COMPUTERS SWEEP UP PAPER TRAIL DEBRIS

Technology has roared like a tornado through the racing office, shoving aside stacks of papers, card files, and race charts.

"When I started, we still took entries by hand," racing secretary Ben Huffman recalled. "We had something called the winner's book, and you wrote it all by hand. We still had the old cut books, too. That's how we produced the program for the printer.

CELEBRATING 75 YEARS OF TRADITION

"Computers were just coming in. Now everything is at your fingertips. It's so advanced, so much more helpful, that it's scary."

The winner's book required lengthy time for an assistant to search three editions of *Daily Racing Form* and record the winners of every North American race the previous day. The large, heavy cut book moved from track to track around Kentucky. It listed the horse's name, owner, trainer, jockey, and silks, and helped a printer put together the 4-by-9 program. "Each 'cut' had all the information, the breeding line, when a horse was claimed, and the new owners," Huffman said. "The new information was cut and pasted for the printer."

The arrival of InCompass, a centralized database that became available to racetracks in 2003, changed everything.

The racing office benefits from InCompass in several ways. Entries are qualified and weights assigned at entry time. Officials can "write" a race in seconds thanks to a condition book template system. Horse lists, such as a starter's list of idiosyncrasies in the starting gate, can be shared nationally. Silks descriptions are stored for easy identification.

"Keeneland is a wonderful strategic partner for just about anything we would want to try," said David Haydon, president of InCompass, which is a subsidiary of The Jockey Club. "We get their thoughts and ideas, and they help us design and build the products. Our role is supporting the racing office."

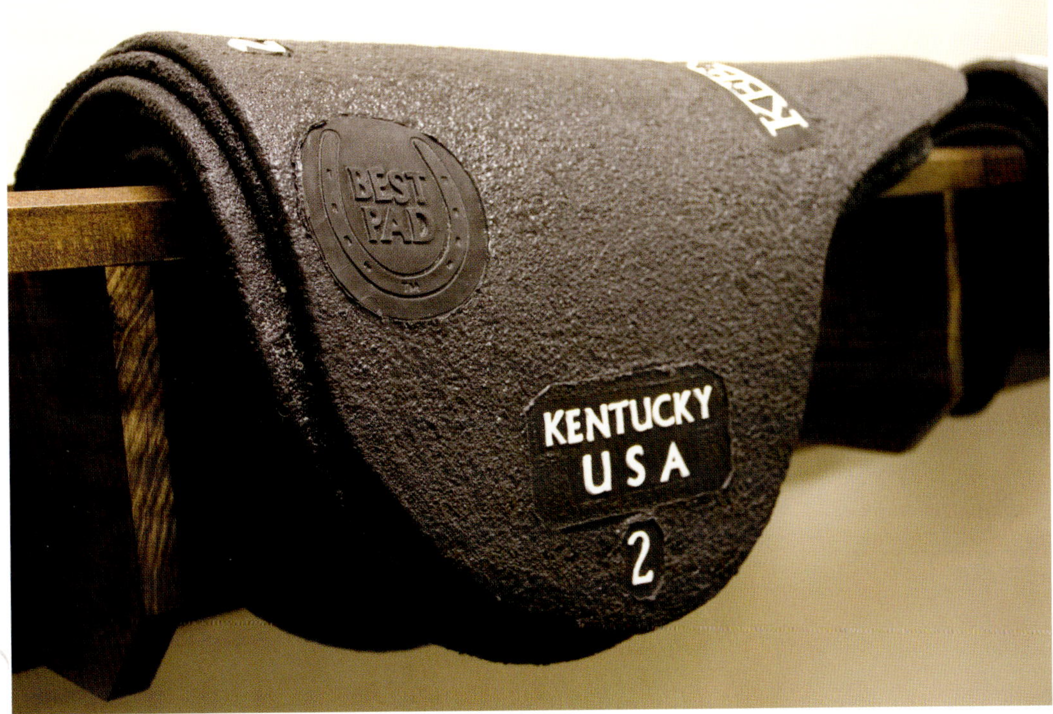

The Best Pad race weight pads require no lead weights and are contoured to fit the shape of the horse.

The Jockey Club Information Systems provides all of Keeneland's sales catalogs. Equibase collects data from race results at all North American tracks.

Other InCompass programs include the Jockey Health Information System, the Equine Injury Database, Horsemen's Bookkeeper, and Pre-Race Veterinary Exam.

The arrival of Equibase has drastically changed the racing program. With Equibase providing past performances and countless other data, the programs quickly expanded.

Today's Keeneland program is full of information and tips to help patrons at the betting windows. Amy Petit, creative services manager, has been with Keeneland since 1981 and has seen photographs of when the pocket programs arrived at the track by helicopter from the printer's office several miles away.

Award-winning coverage is produced in a state-of-the-art HD control room. Keeneland is the only full HD Thoroughbred racing facility in North America.

"Horses didn't scratch until the morning of the race, so it was a scramble for the printer to typeset the changes and get in the morning line," she said. "Equibase came along, and our department was involved with how the program would look and what information we would add."

Today's program may exceed 100 pages. The forty-eight white pages feature the day's racing. The color wrap includes editorial content and advertisements.

"We try to get as much info into the white pages as possible," Petit said. "Trends are big, and we try to include as many facts and figures that are available for the savvy handicapper."

BETTORS GETTING MORE OPTIONS AND ACTION

Hal Price Headley, one of Keeneland's founders, was quoted as saying, "We don't care whether people who come here bet or not ... "

Well, patrons do want to bet, and Keeneland has been at the forefront in making that possible.

Four days before its inaugural card on October 15, 1936, the track introduced a new totalizator, the first to be installed in Kentucky. Previously, betting was conducted by manual calculations. The "new" tote machine registered bets and computed odds and payoffs.

By 1979 Keeneland became only the fourth track in the country to offer a system that allowed bettors to buy and cash tickets at any window. The track now uses United Tote's technology.

Intertrack wagering — the satellite transmission of live racing from a host racetrack within a state to a receiving racetrack in the same state — came to Keeneland in 1988 and soon became a fixture during live meets. Simulcasting — the satellite transmission of whole race cards to out-of-state racetracks — changed the landscape, according to Robert Butcher, director of pari-mutuels. Win, place, and show and the daily double were not enough, he said. "Players wanted more options, more action. It progressed from there."

Butcher said technology has grown rapidly, and he is pleased with United. The company offers self-service kiosks, a new wireless product, and hand-held PC devices.

"United allows customers to have a lot of information at their fingertips," Butcher said. "You can order up specific results from whatever races or tracks we're offering for that day. The machines are a lot faster and more user-friendly."

Looking ahead, Butcher foresees cell-phone wagering as the next innovation. "Customers could have their own personal device so betting would be more efficient and convenient," he said. Keeneland would provide a pin number to log in. The customer would make deposits and wager directly from a cell phone.

Stand-alone machines are available for a bettor to insert cash or credit card and receive a voucher or a FastBet card. "A FastBet card looks like a credit card," Butcher said. "You can load it with money and make paperless wagers all day, while we keep a running tab."

The Internet is drawing customers. Keeneland.com offers PolyCapping, a free handicapping tool with information about Polytrack and turf racing. The track also has handicapping contests with no entry fee; all the money goes back to the participants.

"There's a lot going on even when we're not racing live," Butcher said. "Simulcasting is year-round with different contests and giveaways to attract customers."

CAN KEENELAND LEARN FROM NASCAR SUCCESS?

Away from the Polytrack and sales pavilion, Keeneland's management is at work anticipating the latest technology and innovations. In 2009, Brad Lovell joined the team as director of information technology. Lovell previously had worked in a similar capacity at NASCAR.

Lovell is drawing from his NASCAR past after watching that sport become second in popularity only to the NFL in the last generation. "His experience with NASCAR — widely respected for its fan-friendly technology and promotional savvy — will help us expand opportunities for our clients, sponsors, media and, most importantly, our fans," said Nicholson. "NASCAR is at the forefront in terms of cutting-edge technology, broadcast graphics display, and database use to reach its audience. We are excited to apply Brad's skills in exploring new, innovative means for racing to better connect with its customers."

Bottom line from Team Keeneland is that the best is yet to come as its leaders continually define what racing is meant to be at the historic racetrack and sales arena.

"One of our missions is to push the envelope in a reasonable manner," director of racing Rogers Beasley said.

"We don't need to change often, but we do it right," maintenance director Mike Young said. "Keeneland is not slow to move."

Director of sales Geoffrey Russell commented, "We need to work out how to communicate with all our customers and know it will change tomorrow."

How about in the next hour?

CONTRIBUTORS

Rena Baer is a Lexington-based freelance writer and editor whose work also has appeared in *The Lane Report, Small Market Meetings, Panache,* and several other publications. In addition, she is a copy writer and editor for Roskelly Inc. of Newport, Rhode Island.

Rick Bailey spent the last forty years writing about sports, religion, and entertainment for the Lexington *Herald-Leader.* He is a freelance writer based in Lexington.

Deirdre B. Biles is bloodstock sales editor for Blood-Horse Publications. She has reported on the Thoroughbred auction scene for nearly two decades.

Ave Lawyer lives in Lexington where she is variously engaged in writing, directing for the theater, and providing marketing counsel to a small group of clients.

Michele MacDonald is a Lexington-based writer who has earned multiple awards for her writing. Her work has been published in a number of periodicals in the United States, Britain, and Dubai.

Vickie Mitchell is a Lexington freelance writer and the editor of *Small Market Meetings,* a national monthly newspaper for meeting planners.

Sharon Reynolds has been a professional writer for more than 25 years. Formerly a reporter for the Lexington *Herald-Leader,* she writes freelance articles and also writes and edits publications for business clients.

Erich L. Ruehs is a freelance writer who has done work for ESPN *The Magazine, Cigar Aficionado,* and *Keeneland* magazine and currently contributes to *BusinessLexington.* He lives in Mercer County, Kentucky, with his family.

Fran Taylor is executive director of the Keeneland Foundation and author of *Keeneland Entertains: Traditional Bluegrass Hospitality and Favorite Recipes* and co-author of *Keeneland Then; Keeneland Now.*

Maryjean Wall Ph.D., is author of *How Kentucky Became Southern: a tale of Outlaws, Horse Thieves, Gamblers, and Breeders.* She is a three-time winner of the Eclipse Award and was twice nominated for a Pulitzer Prize. She retired from her longtime position as turf writer for the Lexington *Herald-Leader* and now teaches American history to university students.

Sue Wylie is a Lexington media personality who hosts and produces WVLK-TV-AM's Front Page radio call-in show and is the author of *How To Throw a Great Derby Party.*

PHOTO CREDITS

Forewords: Matt Anderson, 6; Anne M. Eberhardt, 7; Bill Straus, 8, 10; Holifield, 9; Keeneland Library, 11.

Chapter 1: Photos by Z, 13; Keeneland Library, 14, 15, 17, 18, 19, 20, 21, 22, 23, 24, 26; Lee Thomas, 16; Matt Anderson, 26.

Chapter 2: Keeneland Library, 27, 28; 29, 30, 32, 33, 34, 35, 36, 38, 36; Keeneland, 29; Matt Anderson, 32, 35, 39, 40.

Chapter 3: Keeneland Library, 41, 42, 43, 44, , 46, 49, 50, 51, 53, 54, 56, 58, 59; Keeneland, 48, 52;

Chapter 4: Keeneland Library, 61, 62, 63, 64, 65, 68, 69, 70, 71, 72, 73, 74, 76, 78; Keeneland, 63, 80; Bill Straus, 66, 74, 75, 79; courtesy of Ashland, the Henry Clay Estate, 67; Matt Anderson, 69, 73, 83; G.D. Hieronymus, 70; Tony Leonard, 77; Photos by Z, 80, 81, 82; Lee Thomas, 83.

Chapter 5: Matt Anderson, 85, 87, 89, 94, 95; Keeneland Library, 86, 90, 91, 92, 93, 95; Photos by Z, 87, 88, 89, 96, 97, 98; Anne M. Eberhardt, 97, 99.

Chapter 6: Joseph D'Orio, 101; Photos by Z, 102, 111, 112; Anne M. Eberhardt, 103, 114, 116, 117, 120; Patricia McQueen, 103; Keeneland Library, 104, 105, 106, 107, 108, 110; Matt Anderson, 109, 115, 117, 118, 120; Bill Straus, 109; The Blood-Horse, 111, 113; Keeneland, 112, 114; Neena Ewing, 121.

Chapter 7: Keeneland Library, 123, 124, 125, 126, 127, 128, 129, 130, 131,135; Matt Anderson, 127; 128, 133, 135, 137; Bill Straus, 129, 130, 131, 132, 134; Holifield, 131; Joy Gilbert, 133; Photos by Z, 134; Keeneland, 136, 137.

Chapter 8: Tony Leonard, 139; Keeneland Library, 140, 141, 142, 145; Matt Anderson, 140, 147, 149; The Blood-Horse, 144; Charles Bertram/Lexington Herald-Leader, 146; Lee Thomas, 147; Paul Atkinson, 147; Photos by Z, 148, 150, Bruce Sweetman Photography, 151.

Chapter 9: Matt Anderson, 153; Keeneland Library, 154, 155, 156, 163, 164, 165, 168; Lee Thomas, 155, 159, 160, 161, 162, 163, 166; Bill Straus, 158; Anne M. Eberhardt, 167.

Chapter 10: Seabiscuit live action motion picture © 2003 Universal Studios, Dreamworks LLC, Spyglass Entertainment Group L.P. Licensed by Universal Studios Licensing LLLP. All Rights Reserved (courtesy of John Hockensmith), 169, 175; Bill Straus, 170, 172, 173, 174, 176, 181; Keeneland Library, 170, 171, 174; Ron Garrison/Lexington Herald-Leader, 174, 180; Dreamworks, 178; Matt Anderson, 179; Anne M. Eberhardt, 183, 186.

Chapter 11: Photos by Z, 187, 188, 190, 191, 193, 194, 195, 199, 201, 202; Anne M. Eberhardt, 189, 196, 204; Matt Anderson, 189, 191, 194, 196, 197, 198, 199, 200, 203; Keeneland Library, 192.

Chapter 12: Matt Anderson, 207, 212,213, 214, 216, 217, 218.; Photos by Z, 208, 212, 213; Keeneland, 209; Bill Straus, 210; The Blood-Horse/Dave Young, 215

Cover photo: Mike Weaver

Back cover photo: Matt Anderson

ACKNOWLEDGMENTS

We are fortunate to have a great pool of talented writers and photographers in the Bluegrass. Even more fortunate for this project is that a number of them have spent the majority of their careers covering the Thoroughbred industry. We tapped this amazing pool of talent to help tell the story of how Keeneland came to be and the storied institution's first seventy-five years.

We also contacted other people known for their love of Keeneland. Ken Grayson shared his noteworthy collection of racing memorabilia with us to help enhance the Kentucky Association and Keeneland racing chapters. Betty Hoopes furnished early mementos from the Kentucky Association and Keeneland.

The Keeneland Library played a major role in providing photographic images for the project. Those images, in conjunction with the Keeneland Association archives and photos from *The Blood-Horse*, really bring the stories to life. Keeneland's Matt Anderson was tremendously helpful in researching photos, taking photographs of a wide assortment of memorabilia, and working digitally to enhance the quality of the images. Many other talented photographers contributed their work.

Eclipse Press furnished talent and expertise to the project through the editorial oversight of Jacqueline Duke and assistant editor Alexandra Beckstett, the art direction of Brian Turner, and the digital skills of Dave Young. All were a pleasure to work with and helped keep this project on track — not an easy job with so many different people involved. A special thanks to Stacy Bearse, former publisher of Blood-Horse Publications, for his vision in allowing Eclipse Press to take on great projects to educate and entertain those with an interest in Keeneland and the Thoroughbred industry.

Keeneland: A Thoroughbred Legacy is the third project in the series of books celebrating Keeneland as it reaches its seventy-fifth anniversary in 2011. These titles are part of the Keeneland Legacy series. As with other Keeneland Legacy merchandise, all profits from the sales of these items will be contributed to qualified nonprofit organizations through the Keeneland Foundation.

Fran Taylor, Executive Director
Keeneland Foundation

T

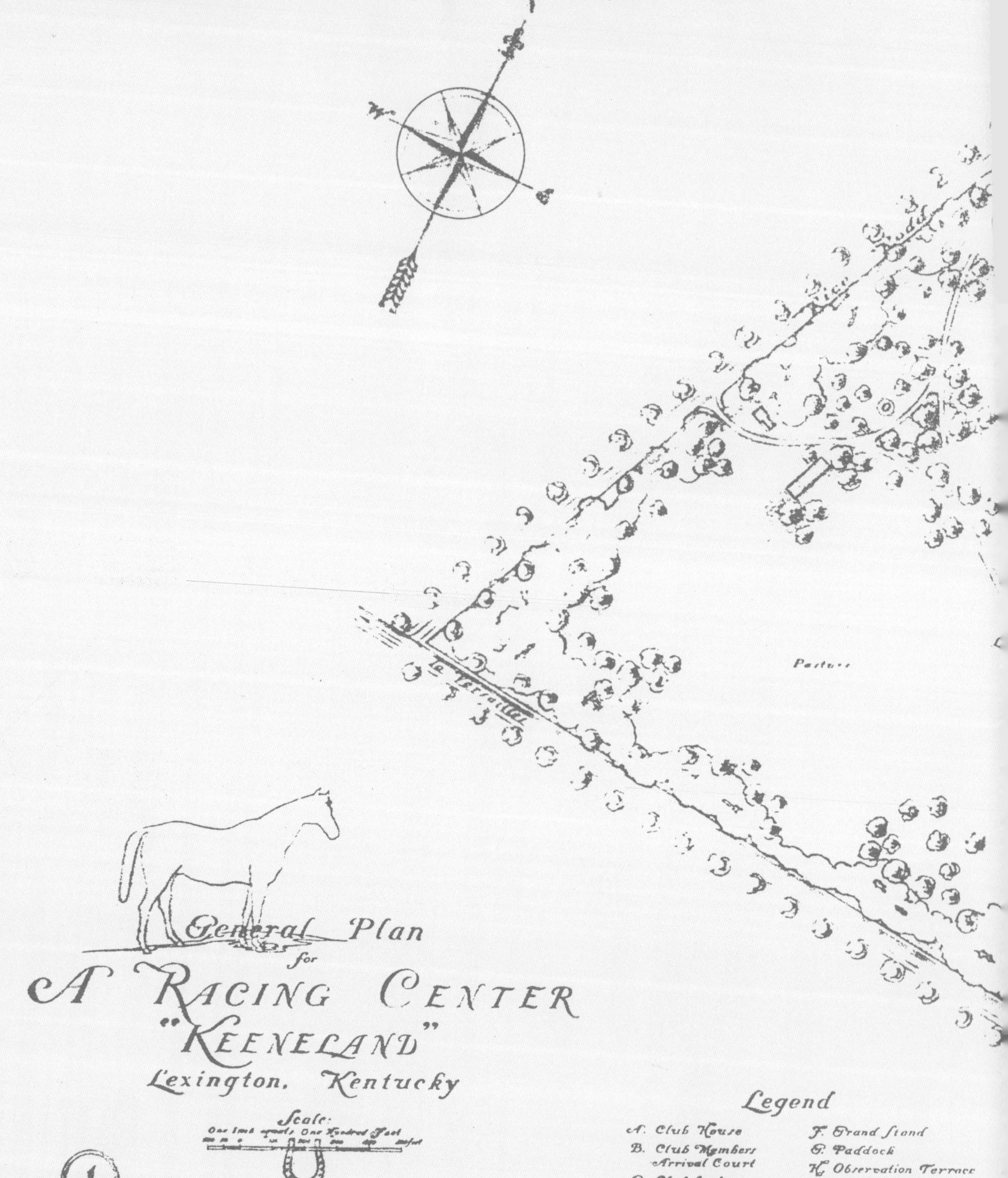

Pasture
General Plan
for
A RACING CENTER
"KEENELAND"
Lexington, Kentucky
Scale:
One Inch equals One Hundred Feet
Bryant Fleming
Architect ~ Landscape Architect
Wyoming, N.Y.
Legend
A. Club House
B. Club Members
Arrival Court
C. Club Enclosure
D. Public Passage
E. Stand Enclosure
F. Grand Stand
G. Paddock
H. Observation Terrace
J. Transportation
Terminal
K. Ticket Island
L. M. N. and O. Future Stable Sites